Uncomfortable Wars

Westview Studies in Regional Security
Wm. J. Olson, Series Editor

Uncomfortable Wars: Toward a New Paradigm of Low Intensity Conflict, edited by Max G. Manwaring

US Strategic Interests in the Gulf Region, edited by Wm. J. Olson

FORTHCOMING

The Comandante Speaks: Memoirs of an El Salvadoran Guerrilla Leader, edited by Courtney E. Prisk

Uncomfortable Wars
Toward a New Paradigm of
Low Intensity Conflict

EDITED BY
Max G. Manwaring

Westview Press
BOULDER • SAN FRANCISCO • OXFORD

U
240
.U46
1991

Westview Studies in Regional Security

This Westview softcover edition is printed on acid-free paper and bound in library-quality, coated covers that carry the highest rating of the National Association of State Textbook Administrators, in consultation with the Association of American Publishers and the Book Manufacturers' Institute.

Published in 1991 in the United States of America by Westview Press, Inc., 5500 Central Avenue, Boulder, Colorado 80301, and in the United Kingdom by Westview Press, 36 Lonsdale Road, Summertown, Oxford OX2 7EW

Library of Congress Cataloging-in-Publication Data
Uncomfortable wars : toward a new paradigm of low intensity conflict /
edited by Max G. Manwaring
    p. cm. — (Westview studies in regional security.)
  ISBN 0-8133-8081-2
  1. Low-intensity conflicts (Military science) I. Manwaring, Max G.
U240.U46   1991
355.02'18—dc20   90-20870
                                                                      CIP

Printed and bound in the United States of America

The paper used in this publication meets the requirements of the American National Standard for Permanence of Paper for Printed Library Materials Z39.48-1984.

10 9 8 7 6 5 4 3 2 1

To the memory of James M. Basile

Contents

Foreword

To a soldier, no war is comfortable. The environment of any type of war is fraught with danger and death on every side amidst long periods of tedium. But, what is meant here by "uncomfortable wars" is that type of conflict which, because of our recent history and the lack of consensus on the threat, challenges our traditional rationale for using national power in support of national interests. The problem is not that conflict in a low intensity environment is uniquely, physically dangerous but that it is difficult to come to grips with conceptually, that it is politically sensitive, and that it is filled with ambiguities that cloud its nature. The chapters of this timely book present cogent efforts to make the understanding of low intensity conflict issues clearer.

To understand the nature of this level of conflict and to seek to respond to it when it affects the interests of the United States or its citizens is the duty of a responsible government. But no democratic government can hope to address these problems without informed analysis, reasoned debate, and considered decision making. It is an important area for discussion. These essays offer the opportunity both to open and to continue a dialogue of this uncomfortable but important field.

Recent changes in Europe and the breathtaking spread of democracy around the world have brought an end, so it would seem, to the cold war. For the United States, this means a resounding success for its post-WWII policy of containment, but it also means greater ambiguity.

Containment focused largely on the direct and indirect threat posed by the Soviet Union to U.S. and Western European survival. In the immediate post-war years and later, the international system evolved from a multipolar Eurocentric condition into a largely bipolar one in which the only serious threat to U.S. and other Western interests was the Soviet Union. This fact made U.S. policy making relatively straightforward. The clarity of the threat encouraged and sustained a consensus that saw the nation take unprecedented steps to engage internationally rather than retreat into isolationism.

There was a cost. Unfamiliar with the nuances of diplomacy, unaccustomed to world power, and given to moral imperatives, the

American public, while supportive, was uncomfortable with involvement overseas, especially in dealing with governments that did not seem to measure up. There was also a revisionist strand in American post-war history that saw the international role of the United States as a dual evil: it lead to U.S. imperialism overseas—the cold war being an American invention to spur economic expansion—while it corrupted people at home. Still, the immediacy of the threat was real enough to underwrite a broad consensus on the main points of U.S. foreign policy.

The intervening years have also taken their toll. Vietnam, Watergate, and now the decline of Soviet power have caused a shift in focus. Consensus is less certain. Meanwhile, the international system has continued to evolve. It is no longer bipolar. It is once again becoming multipolar, but it is a very different multipolarity. The emergence of numerous states, characterized by unresolved internal political, social, economic, ethnic, and religious differences, has created a profoundly unstable international environment. In addition, problems of endemic disease, environmental degradation, and sheer incompetence have helped to render many local governments unable to govern effectively and fairly. Numerous groups with access to drug-related money or other sources of funding challenge many governments and make violent internal conflicts—many of which are inter-nationalized—a constant feature of modern political environments.

The spread of "democracy" to states with little preparation for it has not made the world necessarily more peaceful or less dangerous. The decline of the cold war does not necessarily mean that the United States faces no serious international challenges. The delicate nature of democratization and the vulnerability of a now very interdependent, global economy to senseless violence and spreading political chaos will require close attention. The need to learn to manage and resolve local conflicts and encourage just political order will remain essential goals. In the process of looking to the future, in re-examining America's place in a changing, troubled world, an understanding of low intensity conflict is essential. These essays help to advance that understanding.

Wm. J. Olson
Series Editor

Preface

This volume is part of a continuing effort initiated by General John R. Galvin to revitalize strategic thinking as it pertains to small wars. It evolved from the work of seven practitioners who have been involved in these "uncomfortable wars" for some time. Their work has been brought together to discuss and operationalize General Galvin's call for a new paradigm to fight effectively the most prevalent and most likely form of conflict in the world today—insurgency.

The study of the fundamental nature of conflict has always been recognized as an important step toward success in conventional war. It is no less relevant to insurgency. Given the high probability of the United States being involved in such internal struggles over the next several years, the failure of civilian and military opinion and decision makers to make an effort to understand this type of phenomenon would be unconscionable. This book makes a special contribution to the understanding needed to formulate and to implement effective efforts in the contemporary international security arena.

This book would not have been possible without the active support and assistance of several people. First, formal appreciation should be expressed to the contributors—Ambassador Edwin G. Corr; General John R. Galvin, USA; General Fred F. Woerner, USA (Ret.); Dr. William J. Olson, ASD SO/LIC, Colonel Courtney E. Prisk, USA (Ret.); and Lieutenant Colonel John T. Fishel, USAR. Additionally, Mr. Charles Loveridge, USIS; Dr. Gabriel Marcella, USAWC; Colonel Greg Jannarone, USAF; Colonel George Meynes, USA (Ret.); Lieutenant Colonel Larry Hamby, USA (Ret.); Lieutenant Colonel Mike Patterson, USA (Ret.); Lieutenant Commander Russ Goedjen, USN (Ret.); and Major Steve Donahoo, USA, deserve honorable mention for their help, encouragement, and perceptions.

Alicia Salas and Priscilla Arms did the word processing. Our editor, Aileen Moodie, made us a bit more articulate than we really are. We gratefully acknowledge the professional assistance of these three really sweet persons. Finally, I must also acknowledge that without Bill Olson and Ed Corr beating me about the head and shoulders at every conceivable opportunity, this book would still be in my computer.

It is dedicated to Lieutenant Colonel James M. Basile, USAF, who died in a helicopter crash in El Salvador on 15 July 1987. At the time of his death, Jim Basile, deputy commander of the U.S. Military Group, El Salvador, was involved in a medical rescue mission. His personal life and performance of duty epitomized the dedication and courage of U.S. military and civilian personnel serving in the ambiguous, dangerous world of "LIC." He truly made a difference, and his efforts will not be forgotten.

Neither this volume nor the individual chapters in it should be construed as reflecting the official positions of the Department of Defense or the Department of State. I and the authors alone are responsible for any errors of fact or judgment.

Max G. Manwaring
Panama City, Panama

Introduction

Ambassador Edwin G. Corr

Max Manwaring has assembled and written in *Uncomfortable Wars* a book that should become a landmark and standard study in America's efforts to cope successfully with what is now officially termed "low intensity conflict." Manwaring's brilliant analysis in the chapters he wrote, the superb papers he co-drafted with other experts, and the engaging and significant contributions he selected from other distinguished military and defense intellectuals provide a long-awaited and fundamental paradigm for thinkers and practitioners in this area. At last there is a much-needed base line for the growing body of literature on low intensity conflict, and on insurgency in particular. The book should be required reading for policy and opinion makers concerned with foreign affairs.

This book begins with General John Galvin's prescient essay presented as a lecture at the 1986 Kermit Roosevelt Lectures in the United Kingdom. General Galvin's lecture title suggested the title for this book, as he calls for "a new paradigm that addresses all the dimensions of the conflicts that may be ahead; and for changes in the preparation of military officers that would enable them to adapt to the changed nature of warfare. Describing the changed environment, General Galvin emphasizes the societal dimension of warfare that is no longer fought simply by the military but blurs the distinction between soldier and noncombatant. This expanded concept of conflict involves ideological mass indoctrination and is waged on an arena in which the aspirations of civilian combatants exert an increasingly powerful influence on the military outcome. Galvin points out the triangular nature of conflict today as it involves the government and its armed forces, the enemy, and the people. He suggests that we are moving into a world in which subversive activities, civil disturbances, guerrilla warfare, and low-level violence will grow and multiply. General Galvin calls for openmindedness, flexibility, and a new way of thinking—a new paradigm—in order to understand and prepare for wars of the future in the protection of our homeland and democratic ideals.

1

The remainder of the book is a response to General Galvin's charge. Max Manwaring proposes in the second essay the new paradigm that Jack Galvin calls for, and the following chapters of the text elaborate upon and complement Manwaring's studied and sound model for understanding and coping with organized and externally supported insurgencies. Manwaring's new paradigm "acknowledges . . . that the ultimate outcome of any counterinsurgency is not primarily determined by the skillful manipulation of violence in the many military battles that take place. . . ." Success, according to this paradigm, is determined by a combination of key factors that include but transcend the military dimension. Victory goes to the side that controls best, performs best, and benefits most in the following six areas: (1) establishment of legitimacy; (2) organization for unity of effort; (3) type and consistency of external support; (4) discipline and capabilities of armed forces; (5) intelligence; and (6) ability to reduce outside aid to the adversary. A government threatened by insurgency must therefore wage several kinds of wars simultaneously to win in these six crucial areas. Manwaring suggests that these include war for legitimacy, war for unity of effort, war in the field of propaganda or information, war to mobilize national opinion against subversion, war against outside support to the insurgents in order to isolate them, and military war for operational excellence.

These, I note, parallel in large part the "seven front war" that President Duarte often expounded to me while I was the American Ambassador to El Salvador from 1985 to 1988. Duarte described the fronts as being political, economic, social, psychological, informational and diplomatic, intelligence, and military.

Manwaring's new paradigm is rooted in the reality of recent and current insurgencies, reflections of experienced practitioners, history, the principals of war, sound study, and analysis.

The paradigm extends the number of major actors from the triangle enumerated by General Galvin to war of a pentagonal nature—the government and armed forces under attack, the insurgents, the people, (and added to these three) the external supporters of the threatened government, and the external supporters of the insurgents. War is much more than its strictly military aspect. The military component varies to scope, intensity, and character according to the stage of insurgency and the threatened government's degree of success in the most critical area—establishing legitimacy; which, in turn, is most dependent upon and related to successes in the nonmilitary areas of the new paradigm for war.

Citing Clausewitz and Sun Tzu on the primary need for strategic vision based on an understanding of the "kind of war we are fighting," i.e., the new paradigm and "the right to govern," Manwaring and John Fishel in Chapter 3 examine the cases of El Salvador and Peru. The authors articulate, based on these cases, the long-and short-term aspects of a strategy related to the new paradigm. For the long term, the leaders of the threatened government and the external supporting government (in the Salvadoran case, the United States) must ensure that all their efforts are oriented by correct comprehension that the struggle is over legitimacy, and that all actions are effectively organized by correct comprehension that the struggle is over legitimacy, and that all actions are effectively organized and coordinated around this objective. Strategy in the short term focuses on rendering the internal aggressor ineffective through application of the rest of the principles of war. It demands, most importantly, a proactive campaign strategy, the adaptability and flexibility of military forces, and the primacy of intelligence.

Chapters 4, 5, and 6 continue to focus on the "big picture" and long-term imperatives if the United States is to cope successfully with the changed nature of armed conflict, particularly that which we now officially term low intensity conflict. Bill Olson in Chapter 4 eloquently describes the challenge and frustration of changing thinking and behavior within the American government—with its complex organization, systemically irrational nature, and multitudinous bureaucrats involved in national security. The government and its many components must come to comprehend low intensity conflict, develop national strategy, and efficaciously execute that strategy. Attainment requires living with frustration consciously planning how to change bureaucratic behavior, and translating overall plans into programs. General Fred Woerner, the former United States Southern Command (SOUTHCOM) Commander, lays out in Chapter 5 our strategic interests in Latin America that are threatened by changing circumstances and discusses the need to adapt to the full range of conflict. Adequate response depends on comprehension of the new paradigm.

Court Prisk delves profoundly into legitimacy as the key factor in dealing with insurgencies in Chapter 6. The underpinnings of legitimacy, and therefore the areas to which threatened governments and their supporters must give appropriate attention, are (1) elections, (2) citizen participation, (3) a government's ability to extract and distribute resources, (4) the active or tacit approval of the government by social institutions, and (5) fair and just judicial systems. Prisk stresses that problems arise because Third World regimes may have differing views about the bases for legitimacy. The United States understandable insistence on preconditions, including human rights and democracy, can cause tensions.

Concentrating again on the short-term aspects of coping with an insurgency and again examining Peru, analysts Manwaring, Prisk, and Fishel, in Chapter 7, single out three critical "second-level" factors: guerrilla warfare, the war against subversion, and the war to limit support for the insurgency. Key to victory in the guerrilla (military) war are understanding, training and motivation, and mobility. In the war against subversion it is vital to neutralize guerrilla leadership, develop usable and timely intelligence, conduct effective psychological/public diplomacy operations, and have credible civic affairs organization. To limit support for the insurgency the objectives are to eliminate territorial sanctuaries and to isolate the insurgents from their foreign and external supporters.

Finally, Manwaring and Prisk in the last chapter, drawing once more on insights from El Salvador, argue that the proper strategic perspective for low intensity conflict requires (1) understanding of the nature of the contest; (2) awareness that the legitimacy of the threatened government is the central target of insurgents; (3) unity of effort in the political, economic, diplomatic, social psychological, and military fields; (4) emphasis on intelligence, since it underlies all activities against the subversives; (5) adaptable and flexible military forces; and (6) proactive orientation of the threatened government and its armed forces.

I regret that *Uncomfortable Wars* was not written earlier. I would have liked to have studied it prior to the assumption of my duties as the American Ambassador to El Salvador where Marxist-Leninist-led guerrillas were trying to bring down the democratic government of Jose Napoleon Duarte; or prior to 1980, when I became the Ambassador to Peru, where the violent *Sendero Luminoso* insurgents had begun their terrorism; or prior to 1972, when I was assigned to Thailand, where foreign-backed Communist rebels were trying to build a base in the northeastern part of that country. This book would have been of enormous value to me, and it will materially assist current ambassadors to Third World nations who must deal conceptually and managerially with low intensity conflicts.

The book's relevance may grow in importance as changes between the United States and the Soviet Union become less confrontational, as the situation in Central Europe evolves, and as the world moves from the bi-polar alignments of the Cold War era to a shifting multi-polar arrangement. The acquisition of missiles and other sophisticated weaponry (including nuclear arms) by regional powers, and the re-emergence of regional conflicts could make the international security environment even more precarious. This, coupled with terrorism, narco-terrorism, and continued intra-nation hostilities, and insurgencies could make the lessons of this study even more important for our country's policy makers and leaders.

PART ONE

Context and Concept

1

Uncomfortable Wars: Toward a New Paradigm

General John R. Galvin

We in the military are accused falsely of "preparing to fight not the next war but the last." That criticism is not well placed: we are not, for the most part, obtuse enough to fight yesterday's wars—but we might be doing something worse still. When we think about the possibilities of conflict we tend to invent for ourselves a comfortable vision of war, a theater with battlefields we know, conflict that fits our understanding of strategy and tactics, a combat environment that is consistent and predictable, fightable with the resources we have, one that fights our plans, our assumptions, our hopes, and our preconceived ideas. We arrange in our minds a war we can comprehend on our own terms, usually with an enemy who looks like us and acts like us. This comfortable conceptualization becomes the accepted way of seeing things and, as such, ceases to be an object for further investigation unless it comes under serious challenge as a result of some major event— usually a military disaster.

The Grindstone

The reason we have accepted the comfortable vision of war is that we keep our noses to the grindstone of bureaucratic business and do not look up very often. We are led away from the important tasks by the exigencies of day-to-day operations—husbanding sophisticated equipment, doing the housekeeping and administration, balancing this year's budget while justifying the requirements for next year,

This chapter was originally published by *Parameters*, the Journal of the U.S. Army War College, Carlisle Barracks, PA (Vol. XVI, No.4), December 1986, pp. 2–8, and is reprinted here by permission.

answering the mail. In naval terms, we are keeping things shipshape; what we are not doing is reading the stars and charting the course. We could say, I suppose, that this kind of distraction always must be overcome, that such things as budgets and maintenance and paperwork have been part of the environment in which soldiers live from time immemorial. The difficulty begins, however, when these activities cease to be distractions and instead become the focus of all our efforts.

Things are changing. Think about today's lieutenant, and compare him and his challenges with those that confronted lieutenants in the past. The categories of knowledge are basically the same—leadership, weapons, tactics and techniques, and administration—but there is a monumental difference in what he needs to know about each. He must contend with an amazing assortment of weapons, vehicles, and supporting technology. He is required to keep his platoon at a high state of readiness for combat. This demands his full commitment to individual and collective training, maintenance of his large stock of equipment, and unit administration, in addition to taking care of his soldiers. The lieutenant is consumed by all of this; and while no doubt it is a great education for him, we may be developing a leader who does little thinking about the abstractions, the principles of his trade, the doctrinal foundations of his profession. The preoccupation with day-to-day concerns is not just characteristic of lieutenants; it is true as well of the lieutenant's higher leadership. Colonels and generals fill their time with day-to-day work while professors and journalists are left to think and write about doctrine and strategy. Yet, the atmosphere of East-West confrontation and the level of violence throughout the world make it imperative that we consider whether our military leaders are truly developing professionally or merely performing, working out daily problems. It is a convenient argument that the normal routine of the military life constitutes sufficient training and development, that the leader "learns best by doing". This notion must be challenged. He must go beyond routine and develop, though continual training and education, leaders capable of adopting to a changing environment. The great eighteenth century marshal of France, Maurice de Saxe, recognized the danger of failing to do so. "In the military" he wrote in his *Reveries*, very few men occupy themselves with the higher problems of war. They pass their lives drilling troops and believe that this is the only branch of the military art. When they arrive at the command of armies they are totally ignorant, and in default of knowing what should be done, they do what they know.[1]

The Fortress-Cloister

As a group we have sought a life not only of proud service to country, of challenge, and of adventure, but also one that is a microcosm of tradition, order, hierarchical structure, predictability, and unequivocal response to clear demands. There is an element of the cloister in this, our life of dedication and sacrifice, full of the satisfactions of early rising and hard work—our carefully structured life, routinized, homogenous, full of universally understood symbols.

In this highly satisfying environment, however, we should recognize implicit limitations. Ours is a protected and isolated existence, hemmed in by the grindstone work schedule, lulled by predictability. What is salutary in the cloister is not good for the Army, however; isolation and protection make it difficult to conceptualize, to question conventional wisdom, to look at things another way. Changes do occur within the walls of our military cloister, but usually only when preceded by the long process of consensus-building, in which more time is spent overcoming resistance to change than in examining new ideas. The grindstone work schedule and our cloistered existence too frequently suppress our creativity and over time have fostered generally unquestioning acceptance of a vision of conflict that has not kept pace with the expanding environment of modern warfare. We remain with our comfortable, confident vision of the wars that we might have to fight.

Intrusions

Intruding on this vein, however, are realities that make us uneasy, raising questions not adequately addressed within the existing paradigm. For example:

- Why did the governments of Haiti and the Philippines collapse so quickly? (Substitute Cuba, South Vietnam, Iran, or other countries that have recently undergone rapid political change.)
- Why does the frequency of internal conflict, with its political turmoil, civil disorder, guerrilla warfare, and indiscriminate violence, continue to grow?
- Why have we seen the rise of terrorism over the last decade? Has the overall level of fanaticism somehow increased?
- How involved are international drug traffickers in the conflicts internal to many Third World states?

Surrogate war, general violence, subversive activity, multiplication of small wars, widespread training of terrorists—each of these has intruded on our vision of war. As they have become more noticeable, however, we have tended to view them as being on the periphery of warfighting, at the limits of our set of beliefs about the nature of conflict. They do not fit into our image of war, so we search for ways to categorize and then dismiss them, to relegate them to theoretical pigeonholes where they can be dealt with, preferably by someone else, while we fight the main battles. What we know and understand—to a large degree—is what we have come to call high intensity warfare. Therefore, these other phenomena come to be called "low intensity conflict" in our book, a kind of appendage, an add-on, a lesser thing.[2] This reaction, while unfortunate, is not new; regulars have demonstrated their disdain for irregulars, partisans, or guerrillas throughout the history of warfare.

What kind of war will we be called on to fight? We continue to show our fascination with the ever-increasing conventional and nuclear power of the Soviet Union—focusing almost exclusively on our potential opponent's capability to fight a massive high intensity war in Western Europe. Yet there is no conflict in Western Europe; in fact that part of the world has enjoyed 40 years of peace, the longest period since Europe came of age. The Soviets will continue to threaten Western Europe—but where are the Soviets and their surrogates moving today?

They are moving in the Third World, attempting to outflank the industrialized democracies by concentrating on developing nations around the globe.

Winston Churchill has been quoted as saying, "However absorbed a commander is in the elaboration of his own thoughts, it is sometimes necessary to take the enemy into account."[3] Our doctrine and strategy too must take account of the enemy: to respond to the worldwide situation we must first see that situation clearly. A hard and professional look at low intensity conflict is warranted. Why, we should ask ourselves, does this concept—low intensity conflict—continue to crop up? Why is it so hard to define? Is it a mere appendage to "real war" or is there a closer relationship?

In reality the concept has been present for centuries, and a direct relationship has existed frequently between armed forces engaged in the conventional form of warfare and those fighting in an irregular manner.

Is there some new dimension here, some situation that we do not entirely comprehend? We know that there have been times in the past when far-reaching political change was brought about by a few men under arms. The forces of Harold and William at Hastings, for example, where the crown of England was at stake, numbered under

20,000 men. At Agincourt, Henry V destroyed the power of France with 5,000 men on a battlefield only a quarter of a mile wide. At Waterloo, Wellington's 86,000 men covered only about three miles from flank to flank. Today, the British Army of the Rhine occupies over 50 miles of front. Yet, by the time of World War II, the situation was different. Political change could no longer be brought about by a few armed men. One hundred fifty million soldiers fought a global war in which fifteen million of them were killed. Not only was the physical scope of the war much greater, but such mass involvement resulted in thirty-four million civilians killed—more than double the number of soldiers that died.

The Societal Dimension

Warfare is thus no longer fought simply by the military. It now encompasses entire populations, large or small, sophisticated or developing; and its outcome depends more and more on their collective will, what Clausewitz termed "the popular passion," the compelling motivation and defiant attitude of the people upon whose commitment and readiness to make personal sacrifices military power ultimately depends. We soldiers are accustomed to thinking about defeating our enemy by bringing combat power, primarily firepower, to bear on him. For us, the utilization of any other form of power against an adversary is secondary and supplemental, a lesser consideration. We must recognize, however, that in fighting an enemy today and in the future, even in high intensity conflict, the situation has changed.

We can see this change in at least three ways. First, the distinction between soldier and noncombatant has blurred to the point of being unrecognizable. The advent of strategic bombing during the Second World War showed the difficulty of distinguishing combatants, the strain that this situation can place on social cohesion within a country, and the important role played by public opinion. Second, ideological mass indoctrination has become an important part of combat power, particularly (but not exclusively) in lesser developed societies where some common belief system is a dominant part of the culture. Third, and closely related, the aspirations of the civilian combatants have exerted an increasingly powerful influence on the military outcome. As British military historian Michael Howard reminds us, if this influence is not recognized or if the sociopolitical struggle is not conducted with skill based on a realistic assessment of the social situation, "no amount of operational expertise, logistical backup, or technical know-how could possibly help."[4]

Douglas Pike noted the increased importance of the societal dimension of modern warfare in a recent examination of the Vietnam War. He described two differing perceptions—one view that saw the war as an orthodox (though limited-scale) conflict, another that saw it as primarily revolutionary guerrilla warfare. Vietnam, he wrote, could also be viewed as "something new in history," a "people's war" that

> erased the line between military and civilian, between war and politics, between combatant and noncombatant. Its essence was a trinity of organization, mobilization and motivation in the context of protracted conflict.[5]

It is that form of war, a synthesis of conventional and guerrilla warfare, with greater importance accorded the societal dimension, that appears a likely model for the future.

Military men, however, feel uncomfortable with warfare's societal dimension and tend to ignore its implications. Societies are hard to understand—let alone predict—and difficult to control. Conflict on this plane does not fit our current beliefs about military success or failure; therefore, it is not a subject that we are, for the most part, anxious to pursue. At the same time internal war—in which the societal dimension takes on crucial importance—has become a dominant form of conflict throughout the world. Of the 125 to 150 conflicts that have taken place in the past four decades, 90 percent occurred in developing regions and are best characterized as internal wars.[6]

There are indicators that we are moving into a world in which subversive activities, civil disturbances, guerrilla warfare, and low-level violence will grow and multiply. A number of factors contribute to this growth of violence at the low end of the spectrum of conflict, among them Marxist-Leninist ideology, which calls for political and psychological warfare as fundamental to Soviet success on a global scale; changes in traditional authority relationships; the maturation of thought-influencing techniques in such fields as marketing and telecommunications; the rediscovery of "war-cum-negotiations"; and the general historical trend toward the type of war that involves more and more of the populations of the warring factions. Although these trends have been obvious for a long time, there is little indication that we (or indeed anyone else, including the Soviets) have understood the need for adapting our doctrine to take into account the whole spectrum from low to high intensity.[7] We have not grasped the new environment—the high-low mix—and its new conditions.

French author Jean Lartegy vividly captured the difference between traditional warfare and the situation we confront today.

In his compelling novel *The Centurions*, he portrays French officers turning from defeat in Indochina to face an apparently similar struggle in Algeria. A protagonist in a Viet Minh prison camp contrasts the French and Viet Minh methods of waging war:

> It's difficult to explain exactly, but it's rather like (the card games) bridge as compared to belote. When we (the French) make war, we play belote with thirty-two cards in the pack. But (the Viet Minhs') game is bridge and they have fifty-two cards: twenty more than we do. Those twenty cards short will always prevent us from getting the better of them. They've got nothing to do with traditional warfare, they're marked with the sign of politics, propaganda, faith, agrarian reform. . . . What's biting Glatigny? I think he is beginning to realize that we've got to play with fifty-two cards and he doesn't like it at all. . . those twenty extra cards aren't at all to his liking.[8]

The dimension beyond traditional warfighting, the twenty extra cards, can best be understood not by focusing on the guerrilla and his tactics, but by examining the structure of the struggle itself. It then becomes apparent that indeed we are experiencing something new in warfare, something that requires us to restudy our doctrine, tactics, organization, and training.

The Triangle

The dimension beyond traditional warfare recognizes the triangular nature of any struggle today. In each case in high or low intensity conflict, the struggle involves the interaction between three elements: the government (with its armed forces), the enemy, and the people. This triangular relationship is easier to visualize, and more relevant, in revolutionary warfare. In this situation a government, with its police and military, and an insurgent movement, with its terrorist arm, compete principally for the support of the national population. The insurgent movement—at the outset too weak militarily to seize political control of the country—focuses first on destroying civic responsiveness to the state, and then on eroding the effectiveness of the military and administrative establishments. Meanwhile, the insurgents seek to develop their military arm to the point where it can effectively challenge the regular forces in conventional battles supported by guerrilla operations and terrorism.

During the early stages of the struggles, violence is less an instrument of destruction than a psychological tool to influence the attitudes of specific sectors of the population. The conflict becomes a form of political education that forces a reluctant, basically neutral civilian populace wanting only to be left alone to take a stand in support of the pursued. It takes time, but the insurgent retains the initiative and pushes relentlessly to gain support by discrediting the government.

To counter this sociopolitical challenge, the government must first recognize what is happening and then be willing to acknowledge that its civil support is fragile and its control over the populace contested. To reestablish its political legitimacy, the government must address contentious, long ignored, but popular issues tied to key facets of national life—sociopolitical, economic, educational, juridical—as well as engaging the guerrillas on the battlefield.[9] The resulting burden on the military institution is large. Not only must it subdue an armed adversary while attempting to provide security to the civilian population, it must also avoid inadvertently furthering the insurgents' cause. If, for example, the military's actions in killing 50 guerrillas cause 200 previously uncommitted citizens to join the insurgent cause, the use of force will have been counterproductive.

Military forces fighting a counterinsurgency must, therefore, use other yardsticks, to measure success than the traditional indicator of enemy killed and terrain captured. In El Salvador, for example, the military has come to attach greater importance to the number of guerrillas remaining than to the number of guerrillas killed. The Salvadorans recognize that reducing the size of the guerrilla force can often be pursued as effectively in ways other than just killing the insurgents—that is, pursued through actions that cause the guerrillas to desert their cause, return to their homes, or surrender. Though harder to measure than "body counts," other indicators of success have been adopted, such as the frequency of insurgent defections, the availability of volunteer informers, and the willingness of former insurgents to collaborate publicly with the established government. Such adjustments are essential if a government is to adapt to the triangular nature of an insurgency and accord proper emphasis to the societal element of such struggles.

Conclusion

The education and training of our young officers understandably will be based on our vision of modern warfare. Our current approach, however, does not go far enough. The realities of contemporary conflict challenge us to attain what the 1984 Kermit Roosevelt Lecturer, General Bill Richardson, called "the blend of enduring objectives and tradition together with a willingness to change in the light of changing times." Said in another way, an officer's effectiveness and chance for success, now and in the future, depend not only on his character, knowledge, and skills, but also, and more than ever before, on his ability to understand the changing environment of conflict.

Kermit Roosevelt was a soldier, an adventurer, an innovator, the kind of man who might enjoy a ramble such as this—one that included grindstones and cloisters and new paradigms. He would, I think, be very interested in the question of the societal dimension of war. As we prepare for the future, therefore, we should take note of his flexibility of mind and his versatility as a soldier. Above all, we should recognize that if war comes, we will continue to see involvement of the entire population; this will be true of all war, not simply of conflict at the low end of the scale.

I began with lieutenants, the source of our future leadership, and my theme has been a plea for flexibility and an open mind when it comes to our profession. The defense of our homeland and the protection of our democratic ideals depend on our ability to understand, and our readiness to fight, the wars of the future. Let us get our young leaders away from the grindstone now and then, and encourage them to reflect on developments outside the fortress-cloister.

Only then will they develop into leaders capable of adapting to the changed environment of warfare and able to fashion a new paradigm that addresses all the dimensions of the conflicts that may lie ahead.

Notes

1. Quoted in Bernard Brodie, *War and Politics* (New York: Macmillan, 1973), pp. 433–434.

2. I have no quarrel with this three-part division of warfare into low, mid, and high intensity, or with the British method of categorizing war as civil disorder, revolutionary war, limited war, and general war. (The British manual also recognized that guerrilla war and limited war, and presumably civil disorder all can occur at the same time.) I would also be content with the old method used by the United States Marine Corps, in which the term "small wars" described the lower end of the spectrum. (Eliot Cohen revives the use of this term in his "Constraints of America's Conduct of Small Wars," *Omtermaotpma; Secirotu.* (Fall 1984). All such terms are useful (obviously one has to choose a set and stick to it). We all know that these rather simplistic gradations are needed because we have internal problems of how to divide the administrative work of budgeting and funding, research and development, procurement, and so forth. When it comes to actual conflict,

however, we find that the simple classification inhibits our understanding of what the fighting is all about.

The classification into high and low may be harmful for other reasons. If the purpose is to find a convenient repository for all conflict that is not "high intensity," we may be in for some trouble in terms of our ability to see reality. In the case of Vietnam, for example, early in that conflict we may have invented a "comfortable" war and fought it instead of the real one. We complicated, and in the end frustrated, our own efforts by trying to mold the war to a doctrine that we understood.

3. Attributed to Churchill in Robert D. Heinl, Jr., ed., *Dictionary of Military and Naval Quotations* (Annapolis: U.S. Naval Institute, 1966), p. 102.

4. Michael Howard, "The Forgotten Dimensions of Strategy," Foreign Affairs 57 (Summer 1979), p. 981.

5. Douglas Pike, "Conduct of the War: Strategic Factors, 1965–1968" in The *Second Indochina War: Proceedings of a Symposium Held at Airlie, Virginia, 7–9 November 1984*, ed. by John Schlight (Washington: U.S. Army Center of Military History, 1986), pp. 101–102.

6. Caesar D. Sereseres, "Lessons from Central America's Revolutionary Wars, 1972–1984" in The Lessons of Recent Wars in the Third World, Vl.1, ed. by Robert E. Harkavy and Stephanie G. Newman (Lexington, Mass.: Lexington Books, 1985), p.161.

7. Although the Soviet Union has recognized and supported this kind of people's war as an opportunity to capitalize on discontent in the Third World, there is little indication (in Afghanistan, for example) that the Soviets themselves have made successful adjustments in order to combat insurgency.

8. Jean Lartegy, *The Centurions*, (New York: E. P. Dutton, 1961), pp.181–182.

9. The government must also recognize the importance of managing information directed at three audiences: the public, the insurgents, and influential external actors. There is the "war of information"—the competition between the insurgents and the government to get facts (and propaganda) to the people and important outside principals.

2

Toward an Understanding
of Insurgency Wars: The Paradigm

Max G. Manwaring

Victory in any kind of war—including insurgencies—is not simply the sum of the battles won over the course of a conflict. Rather, it is the product of connecting and weighting the various elements of national power within the context of strategic objectives. Sun Tzu reminds us that "in war, numbers alone confer no advantage. Do not advance relying on sheer military power."[1] The promulgation of such a concept requires a somewhat different approach to modern conflict than that generally used by the United States over the past forty years. The requirement to look for political, psychological, economic, and moral centers of gravity—and operationalize them—may challenge some long-held beliefs. However, if policy makers consider these ideas with serious intent, they may be able to translate moral superiority, battlefield courage, and tactical victories into strategic successes.

A New Paradigm

Even though every conflict is situation-specific, it is not completely unique. There are analytical commonalities in all types of struggle. As a result of an empirical examination of the general process by which 43 post–World War II governments resisted or succumbed to an organized and externally supported insurgency, six interrelated dimensions have been identified as the most salient within that type of conflict.[2] As such, they constitute a model or paradigm that can be used to understand and deal better with that phenomenon.[3]

This paradigm presents the product of connecting and weighting those six most salient dimensions of power within the context of the win/loss outcomes of a sample of insurgencies that have taken place over the past 40 to 45 years. The model predicted an impressive 88.37 percent of the cases examined. Moreover, the estimated R2 (a standard goodness of fit test) equals .91. This shows very strong correlations between the dependent variables and the results of the insurgencies examined. Finally, the model as a whole is statistically significant at the .001 level. That is to say, the chances of it explaining so well by chance or accident are one in 1,000.

The paradigm acknowledges the fact that the ultimate outcome of any counterinsurgency effort is not primarily determined by the skillful manipulation of violence in the many military battles that take place once a war of this kind is recognized to have begun. Rather, control of the situation is determined by level of legitimacy; organization for unity of effort; type and consistency of support to a targeted government; intelligence; discipline and capabilities of a government's armed forces; and ability to reduce outside aid to the insurgents. To the extent that these six factors are strongly present in any given situation, they favor the government's success in controlling it. To the extent that any one component is absent, or all or most are only present in a weak form, the government's success is not likely.

The Principal Components

Legitimacy

Experience shows that legitimacy is the most important single dimension in a war against subversion. The thrust of a revolutionary program relies on grievances such as political, social, and economic discrimination as the means through which the government is attacked. This is the essential nature of the threat from an insurgency, and it is here that any response must begin. A campaign that fails to understand this and responds only to enemy military forces is likely to fail.

As an example, the turning point in the 1950–1954 conflict in the Philippines came with the appointment of Ramon Magasaysay as secretary of national defense. At about the same time, President Harry S. Truman asked Major General Edward Lansdale to act as the United States' military advisor to the Philippine government. Magasaysay and Lansdale understood the futility of militarily taking specific pieces of territory or killing x-number of insurgents—or suspected insurgents. Rather, the objective was the people. In these terms, an offensive was conducted against the psychological underpinnings of the insurgents. The attack was against the argument that the government could not and would not be responsive to ordinary people's needs. By taking proactive, indirect measures to deny that argument, and b y emphasizing the intelligence force multipliers, Magasaysay reduced the revolutionaries to the level of mere bandits within less than four years.[4] This type of counterinsurgency effort was unglamorous and too soon forgotten, but it took over 30 years and a morally bankrupt Marcos regime to return the legitimacy rationale to the insurgents.

Organization

The next factor concerns the government's organization that must be established and empowered to pursue the struggle effectively. Putting this concept into effect would help ensure that all efforts are concentrated on the ultimate common goal—survival. Without an organization at the highest level able to establish, enforce, and continually refine a national campaign plan, authority is fragmented, and there is no unity of effort to resolve the myriad problems endemic to a counterinsurgency—thus, failure.

Ambassador Robert W. Komer has pointed out that this was a major deficiency in the Vietnam war.[5] On the positive side of the organizational dimension—with the exception of the 1966 fiasco in Aden—British counterinsurgency experiences seem to dominate. For instance, an overall coordinator of all military and civil activities has usually been appointed by the British prime minister. A committee of the cabinet provides oversight, periodic general direction, and support of the individual. Normal practice has been to give him the authority to deal with people in his own government and with officials in the threatened country. Together, long-term and short-term mutually supportive objectives are determined and pursued.[6]

Military and Other Support to a Targeted Government

The data show that probably the best possible use of "foreign" military personnel in a Third World internal conflict is one variation or another in the relatively unobtrusive "train the trainer" role. Large numbers of outsiders in a nationalistic environment for any length of time have tended to be counterproductive in terms of the "sovereignty" of the targeted country, implicit acquiescence to "foreign interests," and the consequent "legitimacy" of the incumbent regime.

Wu Ch'i reminds us that "If one man studies war he can successfully instruct ten; if ten study they can successfully instruct a hundred. . . . Ten thousand can instruct the entire army."[7] Examples of this type of military support to a host government would include United States' military training teams (MTTs) turning the first *Casador* (Hunter) battalions of the Venezuelan army into first-rate organizations during the 1960–1964 insurgency in that country. The same was done for the Ranger units that destroyed Che Guevara's revolution in Bolivia in 1968.[8]

All support—military, economic, or political—to a target government must be consistent to be really effective. Examination of the post–World War II conflict spectrum clearly indicates that when any kind of material or non-material support was withdrawn by the United States or any other Western power during a conflict, or when any of this support was provided inconsistently, the possibilities for success against an insurgency were minimal. Conversely, when aid was provided consistently over the long term, chances for success in a counterinsurgency situation were considerably enhanced.[9]

Intelligence

Another factor concerns efforts to locate, isolate and destroy, or neutralize an insurgent leadership and organizational structure. If the appropriate intelligence apparatus and psychological instruments are not in place to find, eliminate, and discredit subversive actions, and revolutionaries are free to exploit societal and institutional weaknesses, history shows that a conflict will continue in one form or another indefinitely.

Yet, most intelligence and informational efforts in the so-called developing world tend to concern themselves with personal enemies and legitimate political opposition groups rather than the guerrilla. Because of this misdirected emphasis and the general lack of concern for any kind of rights for individuals or groups outside the immediate retinue of the "powers that be," motives come into focus and the legitimacy of the government is further subverted. The Somoza and Batista examples in the Nicaraguan (1979) and Cuban (1958–1959) cases are instructive in this regard.[10]

On the positive side of this insurgency dimension, Ramon Magsaysay's efforts are worth noting. Early in his tenure, he started schools to train officers in intelligence work. In those schools, he demanded that all civilians—including suspected insurgents—be treated as well as possible. At the operational level, he took disciplinary action against units that unnecessarily manhandled anyone. Information from local people, informant-nets, interrogations, and patrols increased measurably. It was collected and collated at battalion level and was disseminated through a much-improved system. Exploitation operations, to include psychological operations and civic action based on intelligence gathered at all levels, are credited for bringing the insurgency under relatively quick control.[11]

Discipline and Capabilities of the Armed Forces

A targeted government must generate a well disciplined, highly professional, motivated security force, capable of rapid and decisive actions designed to achieve political and psychological, as well as military, objectives. The data show clearly that the best intelligence and other countersubversion activities are of little consequence without troops who can decisively engage the enemy without alienating the citizenry.

Accomplishing these tasks is no easy requirement. Because serious systemic deficiencies tend to characterize the armed forces of countries where most insurgencies occur, outside help is usually needed. Success against an insurgency requires a willingness on the part of the outside power providing this help to be forceful in encouraging systemic as well as technical improvement. This means linking specific changes with appropriate rewards as a final means of leverage if other, less confrontational efforts fail. This requires a long-term commitment of resources and will. As a consequence, this factor emphasizes building and equipping a relatively small military force structure capable of finding and beating an illusive and dedicated enemy. Numbers and ratios of government troops to insurgents are not nearly so important as motivation, training, and discipline.

As an example, during the 1982–1984 period, the regime in El Salvador allocated most of its resources to strengthen its legitimacy through the implementation of major reforms and the protection of free elections. At that time, there was a good deal of criticism on the part of the political right and from certain quarters in the United States because the insurgents had begun to mount major, conventional-type attacks against the Salvadoran armed forces and had begun to control large portions of the national territory. Nevertheless, the support engendered from the population more than made up for any lack of direct military counteraction against the FMLN (the Farabundo Marti Liberation Movement).[12] Joaquin Villalobos, probably the best known insurgent leader, later admitted that:

> The enemy had already achieved a high degree of homogeneity around the Christian Democrat-Army and Reform program, and they were at their peak in the consolidation of these programs and of their

homogeneity. Only now can we realize that they had reached that point
and achieved those conditions. But at that time, after going through one
of the strongest periods of mass struggle ever witnessed in Latin
America, it was very difficult to recognize the reality.[13]

Reduction of Outside Aid to the Insurgents

The factor in this new paradigm has to do with the separation of
the insurgents from their network of internal and external sanctuaries
and means of support. This requires internal and external political,
economic, psychological, and military effort.[14] To ignore this aspect of
revolutionary war as too difficult and too dangerous in its internal and
external political-military ramifications is simply to deny the
principle of the strategic offensive. A more contemporary example of
the vital importance of sanctuaries is the series of *bolsones* (pockets)
located between El Salvador and Honduras. Again, Joaquin Villalobos
makes the point. "To say that the zone bordering Honduras has no
strategic importance is absurd."[15]

The factors listed above are not exhaustive, but they appear to be
the political-psychological-military elements that determine much
of the success or failure of a given insurgency. They take into account
what Michael Howard calls the forgotten "social" aspect of war,
without which "no amount of operational expertise, logistical support,
and technical advantage can possibly help."[16] At the same time, the
interrelationship of the various components of the paradigm is
stressed. Thus, success is dependent on a balanced effort across the
board.

Implications for Policy and Strategy

The primary implication here is that the various factors outlined
above constitute a series of wars within a general insurgency war. In
becoming involved in this type of conflict, one is not engaged in a
simple war of attrition in the classical sense of destroying an enemy
force or his industrial ability to wage war. Rather, as Clausewitz
explained:

> In countries subject to domestic strife, the center of gravity is generally
> the capital. In small countries that rely on large ones, it is usually the
> army of their protector. Among alliances, it lies in the community of
> interest, and in popular uprisings it is the personalities of the leaders
> and public opinion. It is against these that our energies should be
> directe. . . . Not by taking things the easy way—using superior strength
> to filch (some piece of ground) preferring the security of this minor

conquest to great success—but constantly seeking out the center of his power, by daring to win all, will one really defeat the enemy.[17]

Thus, there may be various centers of gravity within a given conflict, and the primary center of gravity may change as the situation changes. Moreover, success in one dimension of conflict does not guarantee complete success. The more victories in the parts that make up the whole, the better the chances of "really defeating the enemy."

Colonel Harry G. Summers, Jr. (Ret.) provides several illustrations of the dynamism of the centers of gravity in Vietnam. After the Paris Accords of 1973, "one of the first questions (the North Vietnamese) asked was whether the center of gravity had shifted from the U.S.– South Vietnamese alliance to a new center of gravity—the destruction of the South Vietnamese armed forces and the capture of Saigon."[18] Once the North Vietnamese determined that was indeed the situation, preparations were begun that led to the defeat in detail of the South Vietnamese army, the fall of Saigon, the unconditional surrender of the South Vietnamese government, and the final "unification" of the country. In this case, the primary center of gravity changed three times—from the "community of interest" between the United States and South Vietnam, to the classical military force, to the capital city. Clearly, in fighting an externally supported insurgency, the idea of a multifront or multidimensional conflict must be seriously considered. In these terms, the problem of preparing specifically for "counterinsurgency" or "conventional" operations is moot. The problem is to create the ability to be flexible. The ability to react appropriately to changing political-psychological-military circumstances is the key to ultimate success.

These circumstances, or wars within a war, and their corresponding centers of gravity would probably include, but not necessarily be limited to, the following postulates.

First, in an insurgency there is the overriding question of the moral right of a government regime to exist. The root causes of "people's wars" are long-standing political, economic, and social injustice. Until it is perceived that these issues are being dealt with fairly and effectively, the threat of overthrowing a government is real. Thus, the "legitimacy war" is fundamental in this type of conflict. Here the primary center of gravity is the perception of disenfranchisement, poverty, and lack of upward social mobility.

Next, success in any kind of war is directly related to the ability of a government to organize, determine, articulate, and enforce appropriate political objectives for the conduct of the conflict. If a mechanism does not already exist to perform the unification of functions and tasks, it must be created. This might be termed the "war to unify the effort." The center of gravity here would be the cultural, legal, political, and bureaucratic obstacles to unity of command.

Third, appropriate and consistent political, economic, and military support for the duration of a "prolonged people's war" is vital to a targeted government. If a regime did not need this aid, it probably would not be threatened by a serious subversive effort. As a result, another war likely to be fought simultaneously with other related conflicts is one designed to keep an important ally completely committed to the fight. To a large extent this is a "propaganda war" or an "information war." The traditional center of gravity in this case lies in the "community of interest" of the partners against the insurgency.

Fourth, a major concern in any war situation must be leadership and public opinion. They are of even greater significance in "people's wars." The efforts to discredit or neutralize insurgent leadership and create a favorable environment for an incumbent government could be called a "war against subversion." The primary source of psychological strength and balance in this context would be the highly disciplined, trained, and motivated leadership nucleus that tends to make an insurgency a life-or-death struggle for all concerned.

Fifth, outside support is as important to an insurgent organization as it is to a targeted government. The problem here is to isolate politically, psychologically, and militarily the insurgents from their primary sources of aid—whoever and wherever they may be. Like some of the other wars within the general war, this is a conflict that is not necessarily localized within the borders of a threatened country, thus, a "war of isolation," a "twilight war", or "shadow war"—for lack of better terms. No matter what it is called, the center of gravity is the hub of all power and movement on which everything depends—not specific terrain, not supply routes, and not individual convoys.

Finally, there is the problem of conducting the military aspects of an insurgency. Experience indicates that military success is dependent upon well trained, highly mobile, highly motivated, and well disciplined troops. Many times a targeted government is morally, socially, economically, and militarily weak. Thus, even though it might require foreign aid, ultimately, the country must strengthen itself. This is—again for lack of a better term—a "war for operational excellence". The center of gravity is the people of a country. People are the fundamental source of physical, psychological, and moral strength.

In sum, modern conflict is not unidimensional—it is multifaceted. Each part has its corresponding threat and center of gravity. The basic problem is constantly to reevaluate the principal threat and the proper order for the others. The secondary problem is to fight without appearing to fight; to wage war through "peaceful" enterprise; and, to use morally acceptable tactics and doctrine against the enemy. The first definitive step in this process has got to be the full consideration of the entire situation and the various aspects implicit in it.

Notes

1. Sun Tzu, *The Art of War*, trans. Samuel B. Griffith, 1st ed. (London: Oxford University Press, 1963), p. 122.

2. Max G. Manwaring, "A Model for the Analysis of Insurgencies," paper prepared for the Small Wars Operations Research Directorate, USSOUTHCOM, Republic of Panama, 1987.

3. None of the principal components of the model is new to discussions of insurgency and counterinsurgency. What is new is, first, the specific combination of factors considered. Second, the interdependence of the various components of the model is stressed. Finally, and most importantly, this paradigm was not conceived a priori. It is empirically sound and warrants confidence that the findings explain much of the reality of insurgencies.

4. See, for example: Edward G. Lansdale, *In the Midst of Wars: An American's Mission to Southeast Asia*, (New York: Harper & Row Publishers, 1972); Colonel Julius L. Javier, "A Study to Determine the Effectiveness of the Present Counterinsurgency Strategy of the Philippines (Leavenworth, KS: USAC&GSC, 1985); Colonel Venancio R. Duque, Jr., "The Integrated National Police in Philippine Counterinsurgency Operations)" (Leavenworth, KS: USAC&GSC, 1984); and Lawrence M. Greenberg, "The Hukbelahop Insurrection: A Case Study of a Successful Anti-Insurgency Operation in the Philippines—1946–1955," draft monograph by the United States Army Center of Military History, Washington, D.C. June 1986.

5. Robert A. Komer, *Bureaucracy Does Its Thing: Institutional Constraints on US-GVN Performance in Vietnam* (Santa Monica, CA: Rand Corp., August 1972), pp. ix; 75–84.

6. Brigadier Frank Kitson, *Low Intensity Conflict Operations: Subversion, Insurgency, Peace-Keeping*, (Harrisburg, PA: Stackpole Books, 1971), pp. 54–57. A more recent example of such a coordinator having been appointed is found in the Sunday Times of London Insight Team, *War in the Falklands: The Full Story*, (New York: Harper & Row Publishers, 1982), pp. 102–103; 136.

7. Sun Tzu, *The Art of War*, p. 160.

8. These and subsequent examples are based on over 100 *Interviews* with civilian and military experts who were involved in the 43 insurgencies examined in Manwaring, "Model for the Analysis of Insurgencies." The interviews were conducted in the United States, Europe, and Latin America over the period 1984–1987 by Max G. Manwaring and Colonel Alfred W. Baker, USA.

9. Ibid.

10. Ibid.

11. Lansdale, *In the Midst of Wars.* .

12. Max G. Manwaring and Court Prisk (eds.), *El Salvador at War: An Oral History,* (Washington, D.C.: NDU Press, 1988).

13. Marta Harnecker, "An Interview with Joaquin Villalobos," in Dixon and Jonas, eds., *Revolution and Intervention in Central America,* (San Francisco: Synthesis Publications, 1983), pp. 70–71.

14. Manwaring interviews; and "Model for the Analysis of Insurgencies."

15. Harnecker, "Interview with Joaquin Villalobos, p.98

16. Michael Howard, "The Forgotten Dimensions of Strategy," in *The Causes of War: An Other Essays,* (Cambridge, Mass: Harvard University Press, 1983).

17. Carl von Clausewitz, *On War,* Michael Howard and Peter Paret, eds. (Princeton, N.J.: Princeton University Press, 1976), p.596.

18. Colonel Harry G. Summers, Jr., *On Strategy: The Vietnam War in Context,* 4th ed. (Carlisle Bks, Penn. Strategic Studies Institute, U.S. Army College, 1983), p.83.

PART TWO

The Major Components

3

Strategic Vision and Insurgency in El Salvador and Peru

Max G. Manwaring and John T. Fishel

Today political and military leaders are in the process of rethinking the United State's global role and strategies. They are thinking in terms of military reform and the structuring or restructuring of forces to deal better with the security problems that are likely to arise over the next several years. Strategic theory has so far played little part in the debate, which has focused on conflict at the lower end of the spectrum. Nevertheless, it must be remembered that implementing budgets, force structure, procurement, and planning must be preceded by strategic vision.

Before asking the usual questions as to "What are we going to do?" "Who is going to command and control effort?" "How is it to be done?"—von Clausewitz warns the first, the supreme, the most far reaching act of judgment that the statesman and commander have to make is to establish . . . the kind of war on which they are embarking; neither mistaking it for, nor trying to turn it into, something that is alien to its nature. [1] Determining the nature of the conflict is thus "the first of all strategic questions and the most comprehensive."[2] As a consequence, it is incumbent on senior decision makers and their staffs to identify correctly the primary center of gravity, prioritize the others, and link policy, strategy, force structure and equipment, and campaign plans to solving the central strategic problem. This encompasses what B. H. Liddell Hart, drawing from Sun Tzu, calls the indirect approach to war: "The perfection of strategy would be, therefore, to produce a decision without any serious fighting."[3]

In an attempt to provide a better understanding of the type of

This chapter was originally published by *Military Review* (February, 1989), pp. 53–64, and has been brought up to date and reprinted here by permission.

conflict most likely to challenge U.S. leadership over the near to long term, we will examine two supposedly dissimilar ongoing conflicts—those in El Salvador and Peru. The case of El Salvador represents a situation in which the United States has been involved for over ten years in terms of providing money, training, equipment, advice, and much dedication and good will. However, it is obvious that neither the government nor the insurgents are winning or losing. One can waffle on the appropriate terms, but Sun Tzu reminds us that "there has never been a protracted war from which a country has benefited."[4] On the other hand, the Peruvian case denotes a circumstance in which neither the United States nor any other outside power has played a major role on either side of that internal conflict. In that situation, the insurgents clearly have the upper hand—although they apparently are a long way from victory.

An examination of the "strategic problem" in both these cases will analyze some commonalities within the context of insurgency and provide a beginning from which to achieve the vision necessary for success in this kind of "uncomfortable war."[5]

The Threat in El Salvador

The primary objective of the Farabundo Marti National Liberation Front (FMLN) is to bring down the incumbent government and replace it with one which would "see us take power" in order to "make the profound changes needed in our society."[6] This has been stated repeatedly over the past several years. Accordingly, the insurgents' strategy has been altered from time to time in recognition of changing political-military conditions, but the fundamental assumption remains.

The first insurgent strategy was implemented well before the Salvadoran government or the United States determined that there was indeed a problem. This strategy was organizational: an attempt to develop cadres of future leaders, politicize and organize the "masses," and begin the unification of the various "democratic" elements in the country with the purpose of creating a single revolutionary organization for the prosecution of the struggle.[7] The goal was finally achieved in 1980 when Fidel Castro made it a condition for his support.[8]

The second strategy was oriented toward the government. In late 1979, indirect and direct attacks were initiated against the regime of General Carlos Humberto Romero and the civil-military junta that replaced him. The indirect part of the strategy was a psychological campaign to discredit the regime in power and to claim the "right" to govern in the name of political, social, and economic justice.[9] The direct attack came in the form of a limited but "final" offensive that began in January 1981. Buoyed by the guerrilla successes in Nicaragua and armed with more than 600 tons of weapons and ammunition from Cuba, the FMLN leadership attempted to override the preparatory tenets of Marxist-Leninist strategy and take immediate control of the government through the simple force of arms.[10] At the same time, the insurgent leadership overestimated the degree of popular support and underestimated the ability of the Salvadoran armed forces.[11] The result, of course, was initial failure and a rationalization of the effort as the beginning of the "general" offensive that would achieve the final objective.

The failure of the "final" offensive also forced a reassessment of the political-military situation. However, instead of returning to the teachings of Lenin, the FMLN leadership adopted a more military orientation. The decision was made that "there was only one road to victory, that of armed struggle and the use of the people's methods of combat."[12] This strategy remained in effect until mid-1984. During this time, the FMLN retired to the countryside and began to mount major, conventional-type attacks on the Salvadoran military and to control large portions of the national territory to the point where France and Mexico granted recognition to the insurgents. [13]

However, in this more or less conventional-type war of attrition, the forces of the incumbent government had more success in recruiting manpower and—with the help of the United States—more resources than the insurgents. With those advantages and economic and political reforms perceived as significant at the time—such as agrarian, banking and electoral reforms—the regular Salvadoran military establishment began to reverse the tide of the conflict.[14]

By the end of 1984, it appeared that the insurgent leadership had agreed that there had been another shift of the center of gravity. The shift was from the enemy's military force to the source of the force's power and to the external support for the government's reform efforts— that being the political, economic, and military aid provided by the United States. The strategy has thus become one of taking a relatively low profile militarily, negotiating, and waiting for the time when the United States will become almost completely uninterested in the conflict.[15]

The Salvadoran insurgents can be anticipated to continue to focus on two primary centers of gravity—the legitimacy of the regime in power and U.S. political, economic, and military support. They can also be expected to attempt to achieve their ends through political, psychological, and military actions at the strategic, operational, and tactical levels. [16]

In order to discredit whatever regime is in power and to disrupt the community of interest between the Salvadoran and the U.S. governments, efforts are likely to center first on the inability to provide real reform. As examples, the FMLN "war of information" continually asserts that agrarian reform has not been implemented and is a failure; banking reform is a joke benefiting only the government; export reforms are irrelevant; elections have been, in fact, fraudulent; corruption of civil and military functionaries is widespread; and human rights are a sham.[17]

Second, on the diplomatic front, the FMLN continues the war of information at the international level and works hard to be perceived as the only entity that really wants peace and reform. Yet, given their "armed revolution" strategy, the Salvadoran insurgents can only be expected to continue using the Central American peace process and any negotiations for the purposes of appearing legitimate and gaining time.[18]

Third, psychological and organizational efforts with the "masses" have been resumed, not only in the countryside but also in San Salvador itself. Emphasis has been on traditional allies such as student organizations and labor unions. Moreover, the FMLN continues to develop cadres, train units, refine logistical routes and procedures, and consolidate control over border sanctuaries and areas where there is no government presence. [19]

Fourth, the FMLN has broken down into small units in order to continue assassinations, kidnapping, and general terrorism on a carefully measured scale designated to harass and intimidate constantly the population and the government. These tactics are aimed at lessening regime legitimacy in terms of ability to govern and protect the citizenry. In this connection, despite agreements and protestations to the contrary, the insurgents continue to attack transportation and communications networks and the general economic infrastructure in order to sabotage government attempts to do anything that might improve the internal economy and the economic component of legitimacy and also to impress further on the United States the futility of its economic and military aid to El Salvador.[20]

Finally, the FMLN can be expected to mount occasional spectacular attacks designed to give the strong impression that it still has good and relatively strong formations capable of a military victory. Again, this type of effort has its effects in the United States as well as El Salvador.[21] Current FMLN efforts are not primarily military. Any military operation has political and psychological objectives as top priorities. Military objectives are—at least at this time—tertiary.

Thus, the threat in El Salvador—as in any insurgency—is

multifaceted. In addition to the "guerrilla war," there may be as many as four other wars being waged: a war for legitimacy, a general war of information, a war to reduce outside support to the government and a war of subversion. This reaffirms the concept of a multifront or multidimensional conflict and provides warning to decision makers that "the first task, then, in planning for a war is to identify the enemy's centers of gravity, and if possible trace them back to a single one." [22] In El Salvador, the primary center of gravity remains that of the moral right to govern, or legitimacy.

The Strategic Problem in Peru

Peru is faced with two ongoing insurgencies, one rural based, the other urban. The former is that of the *Sendero Luminoso* (Shining Path) and has stirred the imagination of most observers of guerrilla wars, as well as long-term observers of Peru. The latter, the Tupac Amaru Revolutionary Movement (MRTA), with a relatively conventional urban focus, has generated much less concern. But regardless of the specific insurgent groups, Sendero is by far the largest, the most successful, the most violent, and has come to be considered the most serious security problem facing the Peruvian government.[23] Thus, we will focus primarily on that organization.

The principal objectives of Sendero are to gain power and to create a "nationalistic," "Indian," and "popular" democracy.[24] Sendero's view of the new state derives from Jose Carlos Mariategui who was the founder of the Peruvian Communist Party in the 1920s. According to Mariategui, the original basis for Peruvian socialism is the pre-Colombian Indian (Quechua) community. That communal system was destroyed in the Spanish conquest and kept down by the subsequent colonial and neocolonial elites operating out of the capital city of Lima. [25] As a result, Sendero's founder, Abimael Guzman, is initiating a third epoch that will reestablish a truly Peruvian democracy.[26]

According to Guzman (also known as President or Comrade Gonzalo) and in Sendero writings, the organization has planned for a protracted struggle focusing on a rigid five-stage program for gaining power.[27] The first concerns, beginning in 1962, were to establish a dedicated cadre and first rudiments of a revolutionary party, a guerrilla army, and a support mechanism for the entire organization. This would lay the foundations for the subsequent "armed struggle."[28] During the 1960s and through the 1970s, Guzman concentrated on theory and leadership development from within his academic sanctuary at the University of Huamanga in the highland city of Ayacucho, and on expanding his new revolutionary organization's relationships with relatively isolated peasant communities in the outlying districts around the university. As a result of the movement's provision of such needs as paramedical service, farm techniques, and literacy, and of its members marrying into peasant families, it was relatively easy for the revolutionaries to gain both the confidence and the support of rural residents in the Andean highlands around Ayacucho.[29] Then, in 1978, Sendero disappeared from public view.

In 1980—as Peru was returning to civilian rule after twelve years of military government—the movement reappeared. Sendero leadership moved from what they called the "strategic equilibrium" to the "offensive" and began the attack on the symbols of the bourgeois state. Ballot boxes were burned; the larger cities, including Lima were blacked-out periodically; public buildings and private companies were bombed; dogs were symbolically hung from lamp posts; and a series of attacks on and assassinations of local public figures was initiated. [30]

The third, more violent, stage of the insurgency (the generalization of violence) was initiated in March 1982 with a major attack on the Ayacucho Department prison and the Robin Hood-like release of its prisoners. This operation was followed by a series of relatively small attacks against civil guard (police) posts, various public works, and a dynamite attack on the presidential palace in Lima. Then, in December 1982, Sendero Luminoso staged a spectacular event. In an attack on Lima's electrical grid, four high-tension towers were destroyed, causing a complete blackout in the capital and six other cities. Minutes after all the lights went out and everyone was in the streets wondering what had happened, Sendero lit a huge hammer and sickle that glowed from a hill overlooking Lima in celebration of Abimael Guzman's forty-ninth birthday! [31]

At that point, the insurgency had progressed to a stage where it could no longer be ignored. In January 1983, a state of emergency was declared in five provinces of the Ayacucho Department. It was at this time that the civilian government turned administrative control of the "emergency zone" over to the Peruvian armed forces. [32]

Sendero's move to implement the second and third stages of its strategy for taking power took the movement beyond its own core area of Ayacucho. Guerrilla war and counterviolence steadily escalated and spread to other parts of the country. For example, by mid-1984, the state of emergency had been extended from Ayacucho to include thirteen provinces in three different southern highland departments. Sendero is now extending its influence into two other key regions. This is the fourth stage of the revolution—conquer and expand bases of support. Logically, the first region into which Sendero has moved includes the Andean highland departments that extend from

Ayacucho (Junin, Pasco, Huancavelica, Apurimac, Cuzco, and Puno). The second geographical region into which Sendero is expanding is that vast area of the Andes through which the rivers flow into the Amazon system, such as the rich Huallaga valley. This essentially leaves the coastal and northern sierra departments and the large cities under central government control.[33]

This programmatic isolation of the "center" is exactly that. Sendero has won neither the minds nor the hearts of the urban proletariat simply because it is only now beginning to initiate that part of general strategy. The five-point program for taking control of the entire country has not yet been completed. The last stage of the revolution—besieging the cities and bringing about the total collapse of the state—is not scheduled to take place until the interior support bases are consolidated, and the major population centers are either strangled economically or weakened to the point where a relatively small, but direct, military assault would bring about the desired result.[34] This situation may be changing, however. According to *New York Times* articles, and a recent interview with a recognized "Senderologist," Raul Gonzalez, Lima is currently becoming the most important objective of the Sendero strategy.[35]

At the strategic level, then, Sendero appears to be moving toward the fifth and final stage of its program to take power. Thus, the strategy has become one of increasing sabotage and terrorism, taking a relatively low military profile, and waiting for the time when the interior bases of support are well enough consolidated to make the final attack on the "center" a feasible operation. As a result, it can be anticipated that Sendero will continue to focus its primary attack on the lack of the moral right of the Garcia regime—or any other possible rival, including the MRTA—to govern Peru.[36]

At the operational level, the Sendero Luminoso is currently on the offensive. Doctrinally and in dialectical terms, other antithetical activities generally considered "defensive" in nature are also pursued in the "offensive" at all levels. As examples, Sendero continues to develop cadres to man the expanding political military and support components of the movement; to maintain psychological and organizational efforts with the "masses"; and to consolidate its position in Peru's interior.[37] The thesis in Sendero's offensive strategy at the operational level includes—first and foremost—"armed propaganda." Relying on actions rather than words, the leadership chooses to attack the economic infrastructure, local symbols of central government authority, symbols of foreign imperialism, and to enforce its own revolutionary order.[38] The primary purpose of armed propaganda is, of course, to convince the Peruvian people that *Sendero*

Luminoso is the real power in the country and the only "rightful" heir to government.

Tactically, Sendero operates in small units with political, psychological and military objectives—in that order. Examples of these objectives would include assassinations, kidnappings, terrorism, destruction of transportation and communications nets, and the establishment of control over specific areas. All these actions are aimed at lessening regime credibility in terms of ability and willingness to govern and protect the citizenry, and to provide freedom of movement and the security necessary to further the cause. Additionally, spectacular events such as the prison riots in June 1986 are conducted to give the world the impression that Sendero Luminoso is really more powerful and less bloodthirsty than the government and the armed forces, and that even in jail, Sendero is organized to "win" the struggle.[39] Aside from such "shows of force," there will be no direct confrontation with the armed forces on any large scale. Sendero will jab and probe and enforce its will against carefully selected targets, but its primary efforts will continue to focus on the bases of power, that is, the moral right of an elitist, foreign, and non-Indian minority regime to govern.

In sum, the primary center of gravity in Peru—as in El Salvador—continues to be legitimacy.

The Central Strategic Problem

Analysis of a large number of cases since the end of World War II shows that insurgencies and "revolutionary wars" such as those in El Salvador and Peru are wars for moral legitimacy.

That is to say, they are wars to affect the popular perception of the relative moral rectitude of the competing forces. Nations whose governments have achieved moral legitimacy are relatively invulnerable to insurgent movements. By contrast, a nation whose government is or has been perceived as lacking in moral correctness is a prime target for Marxist-Leninist "revolution" and its moralistic egalitarian doctrine.[40]

Thus, the thrust of any given revolutionary program relies heavily on grievances such as political, economic, and social discrimination as the means through which the government is attacked. This is the essential nature of the threat from Peru's Sendero Luminoso or any other insurgency, and it is there that any response must begin. A campaign that fails to understand this and responds only to "enemy" military forces is likely to fail. As an example, General Edgardo Mercado Jarrin recognized as early as 1967 that this aspect of the conflict in Peru would be the key to ultimate success or failure for the insurgents or for the government.[41]

Speaking for the Sendero Luminoso organization, Guzman identifies the lack of legitimacy of all Peruvian governments since the Spanish conquest as the primary center of gravity in the current "people's war" in that country.[42] Jarrin understood the strategic problem and has long, but unsuccessfully, advocated a program to preempt the efforts of Sendero Luminoso. His argument is straightforward: ". . . political considerations prevail over military considerations".[43]

It was also recognized early in the El Salvadoran conflict that the political-moral dimension would be key to success or failure in that situation. Speaking for the insurgents, Guillermo M. Ungo identified the legitimacy of the regime as the primary strategic problem in El Salvador.[44] President Jose Napoleon Duarte understood the problem and countered with a program designed to nullify the efforts of the FMLN. His argument was simple: If the Christian Democrats demonstrate in El Salvador that a democratic system can bring about structured changes peacefully, then the polarized choice between domination by the rightist oligarchy and violent revolution by the Left will no longer be valid.[45]

Within this context, the best that can be said for El Salvador and Peru at this time is that they are not the democracies everyone would like them to be, and they are not at peace. But, they aspire to both objectives.

By transforming the emphasis of war from the level of military violence to the level of a struggle for the moral right to govern, an actor can strive for a total objective, such as the overthrow of a government, instead of simply attempting to obtain leverage and influence for "limited" territorial, economic, and political objectives in the classical sense. As a consequence, the concept of indirect force permits political actors to engage in secret and prolonged wars—striking at an adversary's legitimacy, and appearing to pursue honorable objectives. This can be the case either before a conflict is recognized to have begun or after it has been considered terminated. Thus, contemporary low intensity conflict is war. The tendency is for it to be at the lower end of the conflict spectrum, multidimensional and total.

In these terms, a government (including its military establishment) must meet its contemporary security obligations in three basic respects. First, it must understand the strategic problem and be able to deal with more than the strictly military aspects of "small wars," such as legitimacy. This is a conceptual requirement.

Second, the long-term requirement comprises the principles of unity of command and the objective. Adherence to these fundamentals ensures that all efforts are focused on survival. What is necessary is the organization to coordinate and implement an effective unity of political, economic, diplomatic, sociological, psychological and military effort against those who would subvert a given regime. Also necessary is the ability to accomplish these things and to govern in a manner acceptable to those governed, which equates to legitimacy. Sun Tzu argues: "Those who excel in war first cultivate their own humanity and justice and maintain their laws and institutions. By these means they make their government invincible."[46]

Third, the short-term requirement for rendering an internal aggressor ineffective comprises the rest of the principles of war—the offensive, economy of force, mass maneuver, surprise, simplicity, and security. Adherence to these fundamentals ensures that all efforts center around the appropriate means by which a subversive element might be neutralized. This more immediate requirement subsumes three equally essential elements.

Within the context of the short term, the first requirement is a proactive campaign strategy. The idea is to establish the ability to fight for something rather than react against something else. It must be designed to achieve decisive results; allocate available resources to ensure adequate and sufficient political economic, psychological, and military power at appropriate points of decision; exploit successes; maintain freedom of action; and maintain security.

Another requirement, and the second within the immediate category, is to ensure adaptability of forces and flexibility of actions. The purpose of this subtenet is to enable forces to maneuver successfully against an adversary; implement strategic planning; integrate the elements that constitute power in a specific situation; and articulate clear and concise objectives in order to minimize misunderstanding and confusion in a given situation. This, in turn, subsumes direct and indirect action forces that are well trained and mobile.

The final requirement for the short term is to provide an adequate intelligence orientation and organization designed to establish the capability to strike at a time and place and in a manner for which the enemy is unprepared; to neutralize an opposing organization; and to shift a balance of power decisively. Logically, the best trained, best equipped, and most mobile forces responsible for the achievement of these objectives cannot do so without knowing precisely who is the enemy and where he is located.

If a country such as the United States can understand and implement these aspects of "uncomfortable wars," it will have a better than average chance for success in helping its allies such as El Salvador and Peru in their counterinsurgency efforts. Otherwise, these prolonged wars will grind on, and the United States will have a better than average chance of suffering a series of Vietnam-like defeats, perhaps smaller in scale and less direct, but more debilitating in cumulative effect.

Notes

1. Carl von Clausewitz, *On War*, Michael Howard and Peter Paret, eds. (Princeton, N.J.: Princeton University Press, 1976), p.88.

2. Ibid.

3. B.H. Liddell Hart, Strategy, 2d rev. ed. (New York: Signet, 1967), p.324.

4. Sun Tzu, The Art of War, trans. Samuel B. Griffith, (London: Oxford University Press, 1971), p. 73.

5. This term has been used by General John R. Galvin in "Uncomfortable Wars: Toward a New Paradigm," *Parameters*, (Winter 1986), p. 2–8.

6. "The Role of Unity in the Revolutionary War: An Interview with Juan Chacon," in *Revolution and Intervention in Central America*, Marlene Dixon and Susanne Jonas, eds. (San Francisco: Synthesis Publications, 1983), pp. 41–43. Also see Joaquin Villalobos, "El Estado Actual de la Guerra y sus Perspectivas," ECA Estudios Centroamericanos, (March 1986), pp.169–204.

7. Ibid, Dixon and Jonas, pp. 40–46.

8. On 11 October 1980, the Unified Revolutionary Directorate (DRU) announced the founding of the Farabundo Marti National Liberation Front (FMLN). It was made up of the Popular Liberation Forces-Farabundo Marti, the People's Revolutionary Army, and the Armed Forces for National Liberation. On 11 November, the Armed Forces of National Resistance were also incorporated into the FMLN.

9. Rafael Menjivar, "The First Phase of the General Offensive," in Dixon and Jonas, *Revolution and Intervention* pp. 63–69.

10. Max. G. Manwaring, interview with Miguel Castellanos in San Salvador, El Salvador, 25 September 1987.

11. Marta Harnecker, "From Insurrection to War: An Interview with Joaquin Villalobos," in Dixon and Jonas, *Revolution and Intervention*, pp. 70–71.

12. "Role of Unity" in Dixon and Jonas, *Revolution and Intervention*, p. 42.

13. Jose Napoleon Duarte, *Duarte: My Story*, (New York: G.P. Putnam's Sons, 1986), p.170. President Duarte stated that this was the lowest point in the conflict as far as he was concerned.

14. The assertions made here and below regarding the Salvadoran conflict are the result of interviews with approximately 40 senior Salvadoran and U.S. officials, and with Dr. Guillermo M. Ungo of the FDR, and former FMLN Comandante Miguel Castellanos. These interviews were conducted over the period from October 1986 through December 1987 in El Salvador, the United States, and Panama. A complete list may be found in Max G. Manwaring and

Court Prisk, *El Salvador at War: An Oral History* (Washington, D.C.: The National Defense University Press, 1988).

15. Max G. Manwaring, interview with Dr. Guillermo M. Ungo in Panama City, Panama, 11 December 1987.

16. Villalobos, "El Estado Actual.

17. Manwaring interview with Ungo, 11 December 1987.

18. Ibid.

19. Villalobos, "El Estado Actual" and Harnecker interview in Dixon and Jonas, Revolution and Intervention, pp. 69–105.

20. Ibid.

21. Manwaring, interviews.

22. Clausewitz, *On War*, p 619.

23. The assertions made here and below regarding the Peruvian insurgency are the result of interviews with approximately 50 lieutenant colonels and colonels, and their naval equivalents, conducted over the period 16–20 May 1988 in Lima, Peru, by Max G. Manwaring. These assertions were corroborated in further discussions with other civilian and military leaders during 6–10 November 1989. While they have no objection to the published use of the interviews, these individuals have asked that a "nonattribution" policy be applied to them.

24. "El Discurso del Dr. Guzman," in Roger Mercado U., *Los Partidos Politicos en el Peru*_(Lima: Ediciones Latinoamericanos, 1985), pp. 85–90; "Desarrollar la guerra popular sirviendo a la Revolución Mundial," (Lima: Comite Central del Partido Comunista del Peru, 1986), pp. 82–88.

25. Jose Carlos Mariategui, *Siete Ensayos*.

26. El Discurso del Dr. Guzman, op.cit.

27. Ibid; and, Desarrollar, op.cit.

28. Ibid.

29. It should be noted that the Sendero cadre was largely made up of Guzman's students at the University of Huamanga. Most were bilingual in Quechua and Spanish, and many of them had peasant roots. See David Scott Palmer, "The Sendero Luminoso Rebellion in Rural Peru," in Georges Fauriol, ed. *Latin American Insurgencies*, (Washington, D.C.: The National Defense University Press, 1985), p. 69.

30. Manwaring Peru interviews.

31. Gordon H. McCormick, *The Shining Path and Peruvian Terrorism*, (Santa Monica: Rand P-7297, 1987), p. 11.

32. Peru Interviews, Ibid.

33. *New York Times*, 17 July 1988, pp. 1 and 12; *New York Times*, 24 July 1988, p. 3; *Diario La Republica*, 24 April 1988, pp. 15–17; and *Expresso*, 18 April 1988, p. 4.

34. El Discurso del Dr. Guzman and Desarrollo, Ibid.

35. *New York Times*, 17 July 1988, pp. 1 and 12; *New York Times*, 24 July 1988, p. 3; and *Diario La Republica*, 24 April 1988, pp. 15–17.

36. Manwaring Peru interviews.

37. Ibid.

38. Ibid.

39. For example, see the *Los Angeles Times*, 19 and 20 June 1986.

40. This concept is developed in LTC John T. Fishel and Major Edmund S. Cowan, "Civil Military Operations and the War for Legitimacy in Latin America," *Military Review* (January 1988), p. 327. Also see Barry L. Blechman and Stephen S. Kaplan, *Military Force as a Political Instrument Since the Second World War*, (Washington, D.C.: The Brookings Institution, 1976); Michael Howard, "The Forgotten Dimensions of Strategy", in *The Causes of War: And Other Essays*, (Cambridge, Mass: Harvard University Press, 1983), pp. 101–115; Edward G. Lansdale, *In the Midst of Wars: An American's Mission to Southeast Asia.* (New York: Harper & Row Publishers 1972); and Sir Robert Thompson, *Revolutionary War in World Strategy, 1945–1969*, New York: Taplinger Publishing Company, 1970).

41. General Edgardo Mercado Jarrin, "Insurgency in Latin America: Its Impact on Political and Military Strategy," *Military Review*, (March 1969): 10–20. Note: this article was originally published in Peru in 1967.

42. El Discurso del Dr. Guzman, pp. 85–90.

43. Mercado Jarrin, p. 16.

44. Manwaring interview with Ungo, 11 December 1987.

45. *Duarte*, p. 279.

46. Sun Tzu, *The Art of War*, p. 88.

4

Low Intensity Conflict:
The Institutional Challenge

William J. Olson

The requirements to meet the challenge of low intensity conflict (LIC) are simple. One needs the right people, things, and ideas applied wisely and in a timely, consistent fashion. Why then does it seem we do not conduct LIC very well? Why does it seem that we repeatedly reinvent the wheel? Carl von Clausewitz described the process of why results seldom, if ever, match intentions as the working out of the laws of friction. Everything is simple, but even the simplest of things is difficult. In order to do anything in LIC, one must begin with this understanding.

One must also understand that there are three key points that must be balanced in order to develop and sustain an effort. First, one must have a good grasp of the particular characteristics of a given LIC situation. Although there may be similarities in events in different areas and at different times, the dissimilarities and unique aspects must be understood as well. This means careful, ongoing analysis not only of the situation but also of one's own paradigms and mental frameworks to be sure that these are flexible and grounded in reality.

Second, one must appreciate that there is, apart from the objective circumstances of a particular LIC situation, a policy formation and execution environment, including domestic and international public opinion that responds to its own internal tempo and imperatives. Since many LIC environments involve the United States as well as host nations, the policy environment is doubly complex.

Third, in responding to LICs, one must remember that it is a dynamic, reactive context. In an insurgency, for example, there is an

This chapter was originally published by *Military Review* (February, 1989), pp. 6–17, and has been reprinted here by permission.

opponent who responds to our actions, or forces us to respond to his. This is an opponent capable of analyzing policies and actions aimed at him and of devising responses to frustrate them. As Winston Churchill once observed, it is sometimes necessary to take the enemy into consideration in one's thinking. The best crafted concepts do not come packaged with a guarantee of success.

Of these three points, the one that requires the most effort to appreciate is the second. Although the policy formation structure is designed to relate actions to intentions, if one stops with this as an interpretation of what goes on within it, then one is likely to be continually surprised when the structure seems to frustrate intentions or pursues actions unrelated to circumstances. While reform is possible, many of the characteristics discussed below are inherent in the process. Since they cannot be eliminated, only modulated, it is essential to understand the elements in order to proceed.

Systemic Irrationality

Since 1945, the United States has used force or the threat of force to protect its interests over 500 times, mostly in the Third World. Virtually all of these have been LIC situations, many of them involving multiyear U.S. commitments. Yet, it seems that each of these is treated as if it were the first time we ever had to deal with an LIC situation and the first time we had to think about it. Responses have tended to be ad hoc, piecemeal, and sui generis. This is not to say that there are not sudden, dramatic situations requiring crisis management, but rather that crisis management is not policy, and that long-term situations do not respond well to management by exception. It is not easy, however, for our political system—or any other, for that matter—to respond well to the demands posed by LIC. The answer to why this is so lies in the nature of the institutions through which we must work in order to achieve results.

Complex institutions and bureaucratic systems are the result of evolution and a response to organizing human behavior in a systematic way in order to deal with large, complex, multifaceted problems that go beyond what individuals or uncoordinated actions can hope to handle. While the development of such complex systems has permitted considerable increases in organizations to deal with ever more complex problems, it carries with it certain costs, among these inherent characteristics that make it difficult to respond well to certain types of problems.

It should be remembered that one of the ways complex systems work is to simplify and routinize, as far as possible, the components of decision making in dealing with complex issues. This is a perfectly rational response and works 90 percent of the time, but problems that fall outside the routine, as Ambassador Robert W. Komer so eloquently noted, tend to be ignored or forced into familiar patterns that bear little relationship to the needs of the situation. That this is so can also be the result of the focus of the complex institutions in question, the scale of the considerations, and the habits that develop for responding to the world.

The United States, for example, has spent most of the post–World War II period focused on the Soviet threat. The centerpiece of foreign policy and military strategy has been the effort to deal with what is perceived as an exceptionally pressing and enduring threat to national survival, both directly and indirectly. Influence goes where money and manpower are put. With 40 years of focus, the lion's share of money and effort in U.S. foreign and military planning has gone to coping with the Soviets, with all the institutional habits and careers that this has created. Further, the American public is not particularly comfortable with a U.S. international role, and it has been the overwhelming Soviet threat that has won its support for nonisolationist policies. Thus, political support and rhetoric reinforce the focus on the Soviets.

The scale of this concern has created institutions, planning systems, force structures and training designed to respond to the possibilities of major war with the Soviets and a policy aimed at using our strength so developed to deter such possibilities. All of this has imparted momentum or inertia to a way of institutional response. It is extremely difficult to shift such an orientation, and more so if one factors in the distinct likelihood that the effort to change this focus will not produce more and better attention to LIC, for example, but will simply reinforce isolationist sentiments and a major retrenchment. Few institutions are willing to sacrifice themselves or programs that have represented institutional life for a generation for efforts that are alien or likely to represent a loss of function. Blind attempts to effect changes in such an environment are likely to elicit an equally blind, negative reaction even if the changes are logical, realistic, and inexpensive.

The development of a consensus and a view of priority are also inherent in the evolution of institutional focus and habit. Whether conscious or not, decision making generally occurs in consensual context, growing out of a paradigm or framework of analysis. The stronger the consensus, the more resistant are institutions to acknowledging or accepting contrary views, even in the face of compelling evidence—and in the case of LIC, the evidence is ambiguous and therefore open to conflicting interpretation. Further, a sense of priority grows out of consensus, a view of what is or is not important. Since this view is spread across the institution and across time and is shared by a number o f people, it is not a simple undertaking either to challenge this sense of priority or to win acceptance of an alternative view. In an environment where views and priorities clash, the resolution is generally a bartered—not adirected—process. This means that no one possesses sufficient authority to direct an answer; thus, decisions are reached by compromise and trade-off. The result is often the most possible solution, not the best possible—if viewed in the abstract.

Systemic irrationality, then, is inherent in the decision-making process in complex institutions. In the case of decision making for U.S. national strategy, the number of players—institutional and individual—is so large and varied that it is hard to keep track of what is happening and easy to form the opinion that nothing is happening.

The Development of National Strategy

There are two steps in the development of strategy: its articulation, words on paper; and its execution, the process of taking fine sentiments and translating these into meaningful action. Neither is a very straightforward process. Strategy conception grows out of a number of sources. It is the result of the prevailing ideas of national interest, the interpretation of this by the administration in office, the public climate of the day and an assessment of the situation and the resources needed—and available—to respond. Since there are any number of potential conflicts in priority in this process, the conception of strategy and of the strategic environments is involved in arbitration before it receives serious focus. Once a decision is made to develop a strategy in a particular area, the process becomes quite complex.

If the president, for example, determines we need a national strategy for country "A", his statement must be worked out in detail to have meaning. This requires time and interagency coordination—the more complex the issue, the more coordination and time. A typical evolution can require the participation, at various levels, of the National Security Council, the State Department, the Department of Defense, the Central Intelligence Agency, the Treasury Department, the Commerce Department, the Office of Management and Budget, the Justice Department, and the Department of Energy. Since each of these is composed of components that must have a say in the process if the product is to reflect the breadth of interests and issues involved, they too must be coordinated, their views developed and arbitrated. Each agency involved in the process has its own methodology for approaching problems and individual views on the nature of the solution. These differences must be accommodated and reconciled. Thus, considerable activity accompanies the mere articulation of a strategy, and the process as outlined here does not include the need to respond to changes in the environment—elections, the views of Congress, the impact of public opinion—which may significantly alter the proceedings.

Once a strategy is developed conceptually, it must then be translated into appropriate action, a process quite different from that involved in developing the strategy, but one no less complex. In addition, another factor must be incorporated—whether the situation involves short- or long-term responses. The shorter the cycle involved, the closer the situation is to a crisis and the more truncated the decision-making process; that is, the less time it takes to reach a decision. Things happen a lot faster. But since every situation is not a crisis and cannot be treated as such, there is also a need for long-term policy development. The longer the cycle, however, the more involved is the coordination process, because there are more interests that must be accommodated.

In the case of country A, if the situation is a crisis, many elements of decision making can be foreshortened—although such a process may have little to do with strategy as compared to crisis management. If, however, the requirement is what to do to secure the country's long-term stability, then the complex process of translating strategy into appropriate action is engaged. Leaving aside the coordination issue for the moment, the immediate problem is how to reconcile time frames and frames of reference. An analogy might make this clearer.

On the battlefield, there is a distinct difference in the time scale and frame of reference of the overall commander and his component commanders, particularly his company and platoon leaders. For a squad, the "battle" is localized and immediate, and it may be over very quickly, in minutes or hours. The decisions are related to the immediate situation. For the overall commander, the battle may take days or weeks, and events at any one locale may or may not be decisive in the ultimate outcome, and decisions are less connected to localized issues. At the scene, there is a more direct, real-time connection between decisions and actions than at various levels removed from the immediate problem—which is perceived differently at various levels of engagement and perspective. Yet, the local commander's decision-making ability and even the nature of the problem he faces may be determined by the overall commander's decisions, those of the opponent, and the evolution of the situation—circumstances removed in time and place from the immediate scene. In such a "dysynchronous" environment there are rich opportunities for confusion, conflicts of purpose and misinterpretation.

The local commander may conclude that his overarching guidance is at variance with the objective situation, requiring a new course of action, or at least interpretation and individual initiative. This may be rational in his situation and totally at odds with the logic and demands of the overall situation. The reverse can also be true. An appreciation of the "big picture" may totally blind higher-level commanders to demanding realities at the points of engagement. Further, there may be no time, at any level, to absorb all the information or no mechanisms for adequately accumulating and interpreting the flow of information that may be contradictory. To subordinate commanders, decisions from on high may appear foolish—may be foolish by local terms—while actions by subordinates may seem insubordinate to higher levels. Better or faster communication is not likely to resolve this issue; in fact, it can make problems worse.

The result of dysynchronous time is that the higher commander is often out of touch with localized events and must rely upon a system of centralized planning and decentralized execution. He must make his intentions clear, lay down the direction and terms of reference, and then trust his subordinates—who are in contact with local reality—to take the steps necessary to adjust to events. A sound principle of management or leadership, expressed in Peter F. Drucker's book, "Management: Tasks, Responsibilities, Practices", is to understand that:

> A decision should always be made at the lowest possible level and as close to the scene of action as possible. However, a decision should always be made at a level insuring that all activities and objectives are fully coordinated.

This ought to be the case, since virtually everyone subscribes to theory Y—leadership. That is, everyone believes it in principle. They especially believe it should apply for their higher authorities. In practice, however, especially with the advent of more and better communications, everyone is a practitioner of theory X—micromanagement. The result is that the higher commander is no longer out of touch with his local subordinates. He is still out of touch with local reality, but modern communications give him the instantaneous ability to intervene in circumstances of blissful ignorance or misperception. Thus, the higher commander can become directly involved. This "over" command, control, and communication tends to convert the functions of the higher authority into that of each of its many local components—robbing higher authority of perspective and the time to think about the larger issue, and depriving the local authority of the independence of action needed to respond with flexibility to rapidly changing circumstances.

All of these problems exist in the policy decision-making environment as well; therefore, it is sometimes easy for local authorities to perceive a lack of policy from higher up, while higher authorities sometimes miss the meaning of the principle of centralized planning execution. Further complicating the picture, the pace of local events is quite different from that in the policy environment. While the centralized planning effort is very deliberate, often cumbersome, and slow, local events can move or change quickly. Consensus takes time, and effective policy generally requires a fair amount of agreement. Moreover, something else has complicated the picture, relating to theory X versus theory Y concepts.

Given the political sensitivity of most foreign policy issues—the use of force in local circumstances, for example, can produce adverse public reactions in the United States and embarrass the leadership—joined with improved communications, policy makers have tended to become action officers and operators. On the one hand, this is understandable. In a foreign country, local events can have immediate and significant strategic and political implications that are beyond the ability of local authorities, while they involve political concerns at home that are every bit as pressing as those situations unfolding on the scene. Problems may also fall outside any existing policy or contingency planning. Such a situation can, of course, mean direct and immediate guidance from above. On the other hand, the result of involvement from above can be disruptive to the whole principle of centralized planning and decentralized execution. It breeds frustration and mistrust at top and bottom, and it blurs the distinction between thinking and doing. The result can be the ready-fire-aim principle of response. Senior leadership becomes increasingly absorbed in day-to-day micromanagement. Everything becomes "hot," a crisis. Everyone must be informed and involved. Everything becomes a choice between now and not now, and only the now counts. Policy making cannot keep up, and even when policy exists, it is often ignored or events make hash of it.

There is a further time component that can fuel impatience and misperception. Presumably, on the battlefield the forces involved come equipped with doctrine and the necessary equipment. These were decided upon and developed before the engagement. In the policy environment, however, doctrine may have to be devised along with

the strategy, and even if this is not the case, there is a lengthy process
to communicate and to "sell" the strategy concept to all the constituent
elements that must implement it. It has taken three years, for
example, to sell LIC doctrine. This process must compete with other
demands on time and quite possibly overcome institutional opposition
if it flies in the face of practice or accepted procedure. All of this
means that the execution phase can be attenuated, giving the
impression to harried officers in the field that there is no policy or
strategy. Thus disillusioned, they often improvise, a process that is
understandable but one that can seriously distort or delay the
development of strategy and convince senior leaders that local
authorities are not to be trusted without constant supervision. A
vicious cycle develops of uncoordinated localized actions and of
centralized control and increasing micromanagement to force local
action to conform, and so on. The real problem lies in dysynchronous
time and conflicting perspectives, for which there are no easy
solutions.

Personnel turbulence only compounds this difficulty. At the highest
levels, the comings and goings of key people can mean abrupt shifts in
goals and lengthy reevaluations of efforts. At lower levels, it can mean
loss of memory—a key player leaves and no one is there to pick up the
effort. If these difficulties were not enough, there is a further
dilemma, one that lies at the very heart of even trying to analyze the
issues that are at stake.

Anyone who has ever observed others play chess will immediately
recognize the puzzle. Standing outside the game, one always sees what
the players should do but miss because they lack perspective. For the
players, it is difficult to see a problem or evaluate it accurately when
in the middle of it, engaged in a situation that can make nonsense of
efforts, however well conceived. Yet, remaining aloof offers no out
either; for the observer has no stake in the game and therefore holds
opinions not grounded in the circumstances or subject to testing by the
reality of the game. One must also allow for the discrepancy between
knowing and doing.

Knowing about something does not tell one what to do about it or
guarantee success, and the ability to conceive outcomes is not directly
related to the actions required to achieve outcomes that occur in a
contingent reality, in a resistant medium. Operators do not have time
to conceive policy in order to act, and policy makers do not have the
time to absorb the lessons of myriad immediate actions and translate
these into coherent policy. Thus, in the national strategy environment
it becomes quite difficult to relate intentions to actions quickly or
consistently. In other words, conception moves at the speed of light,

while implementation moves at the speed of a Missouri mule with colic.

Living with Frustration

If this dismal picture is accurate, it would appear that the only rational choice is to go fishing. Nothing is doable and nothing gets done. But this is not the case. Frustration comes not from being unable to achieve results but from expecting reality to live up to imagination; of expecting to get 110 percent of what one wants and being unwilling to accept less; from being impatient and unwilling to accept setbacks as part of the process; from wanting to fight rather than win. We may not be able to control circumstances but we can influence them. Chance, Louis Pasteur noted, favors the well prepared. Being right does not suffice. The evolution of LIC concepts is a case in point.

Most people will acknowledge that the LIC situation—ranging from peacetime contingency operations, counterterrorism and peacekeeping operations, to foreign internal defense—is the conflict environment in which the United States has been most engaged since World War II, and that it is the most likely threat environment of the future. Yet, policy development, strategic planning, force design, equipment acquisition, and doctrine have tended to focus on major conventional war and above. Many of the capabilities required in LIC are low priority, are not career enhancing, and have been allowed to atrophy or decay. Beyond the Defense Department, there is resistance to the concept altogether, LIC being viewed as solely a defense program. Even the term is subject to dispute. We are told we need a new one because this one is confusing or not exact enough. We have worked our way through a blizzard of synonyms and definitions since world War II, and none of them has made the subject any clearer or easier to deal with, but we still search for the magic words, hoping in their incantatory powers.

The difficulties in getting acceptance of the need to develop policies and strategies for the LIC threat environment, in painfully reassembling the lessons learned from past and capturing new ones, and in reinstituting capabilities to respond have led some ardent supporters of LIC to assume that there is a vast conspiracy to keep anything from happening. This has added yet another contentious component to an already sensitive issue. It has led some to feel that the LIC concept, while not invalid, is a conspiracy of a few careerists to divert, for personal aggrandizement, attention and resources away from more serious issues—or at least to threaten all important issues of turf. Perhaps it is inevitable, but the result has been to emotionalize a complex problem and convert much of the discussion into a question of who is right rather than what is right.

Despite this, a great deal has, in fact, happened. To name only a few: there is a definition for LIC and a national strategy signed by the president; there is a board for LIC; there has been a dramatic increase in course time at almost all service schools and colleges; there is continuing high-level interest in the need for effective LIC strategies; and there is an effort to develop service and joint doctrine for LIC. It remains a subject of discussion and debate. The terminology has also spread beyond the narrow circles of the U.S. government. Soviet General Secretary Mikhail S. Gorbachev has used it, and many of the left and in Communist circles have begun to employ the term—though these latter efforts completely misconstrue, for their own purposes, the purport and natures of the subject. Overall, significant progress has been made in a few years, although much of it is recovering lost ground, and much remains to be done.

What Is to Be Done?

People ought to practice what they preach. If LIC is the most likely source of threat to U.S. interests, where is the corresponding effort to deal with it? If theory Y (or any alternate) is the accepted view for proper management, where is the individual and institutional self-discipline and trust necessary to make it work? If we believe in the importance of long-term policy and strategy, where is there corresponding patience and commitment to seeing something through? It is not likely that these contradictions will receive magical resolution. They have grown from inherent features of our systems and also from a deep distrust in ourselves and others that has come to pervade our thoughts in recent years. It is doubtful that we can change this, at least soon, but fortunately, we do not have to shoulder this whole immense load and stagger about under its debilitating weight. Besides, if Murphy's law is right, circumstances are always against us. We face Hamlet's dilemma: "To be or not to be . . . to suffer the slings and arrows of outrageous fortune, or to take arms against a sea of troubles, and by opposing, end them."

We can act, and by acting—based on sound thinking and planning—help to control what happens. Chance favors the well prepared.

First, one must approach the policy-making environment with a strategy. If it is important to have a plan to implement policy, it is equally important to think through what one must do to achieve the policy and strategy in the first place. These are not the result of right prevailing, but of a series of seemingly endless conflicts. It is as vital to know this battlefield as any other. Second, one must have a sense of how long things take, of what to take on and in what order, and of the battles that have to be lost. Everyone can tolerate winning, but it is important to know when and how to lose. Finally, one must have patience and persistence. "If at first . . ."

There are also a number of concepts to bear in mind. First, no matter the level involved (or the subject), the process to get something done must be understood. Accomplishing anything involves a constellation of players, competing interests, and differing methods and motives. These must be comprehended. Second, long-term issues require a support environment that builds and sustains consensus and a constituency. This environment must be developed—through discussion, debate, papers, conferences, public efforts—and continually nurtured. Ideas are like movie stars; they vanish without attention. Third, the more players (institutional or individual) in favor of an issue, the harder it is to stop an idea; the converse is also true. Fourth, it is important to develop an understanding of short cycles and long cycles. Actions, for example, are short term, even if they are taken as part of efforts to realize long-term goals. Concepts and ideas are long term; that is, they take significant investments of energy over time to realize. The development of things—equipment, research and development—is also long term. Without a sense of time and timing one can make, one can lost sight of what is appropriate to the circumstances.

To translate these conceptions into a program also requires a number of discrete understandings. One must know when to and when not to "hot wire" the system. This generally only works on short-term issues; that is, in a crisis. Complex systems have complex methodologies of doing business. These methodologies may appear—may be—ponderous, and sometimes it is necessary to short-circuit them. However, a continual practice of doing so, although this may produce gratifying immediate personal results, generally undermines the ultimate effort and frequently produces a backlash that destroys it and everything associated with it, guilty or not. It is important to know where to begin an effort, where in the chain to go for coordination, approval, advice, or support. This may require several diverse starting points. It is essential to know as much about the agendas—yours, other people's, personal and institutional—as possible. One must know when, where, how, and in what format to present issues and how to redirect effort, especially for long-cycle issues. To deal with complex problems, it is not individuals who respond but institutions. Thus, how institutions earn and employ what they learn must become the focus of effort. This requires building a constituency and acquiring authority—long cycles.

The LIC Effort

People, things, and ideas . . . mostly people . . . and people first—
that is what the LIC effort requires. But how to get there from here,
that is the question. Patience and hard work are called for, along with
a tolerance for frustration. The ingredients are reasonably simple. In
order to get good people, you have to recruit them, train them, give
them meaningful assignments, promote them, and reward them. This
requires a system for training and tracking, and it requires an emphasis
on doing so for LIC. Acquiring things needs an understanding of what is
appropriate, when, where, and how much. It requires a system attuned
to the external realities as much as to its own imperatives. Developing
ideas demands thought and thoughtfulness, a willingness to learn from
(or unlearn) past successes and failures—a singularly troublesome
thing to do—and a habit of relating ideas to actions. This requires a
system for collecting and evaluating information and for turning the
product of this study into meaningful policy. These all require careful
integration, balanced application, and understanding. Knowing is not
enough.

Nor is any of this sufficient if the will is lacking—personal,
institutional, or national. Results are the product of effort and
commitment. As noted earlier, there are many—here and abroad—
who actively oppose U.S. commitments overseas and the need for a LIC
policy. Indeed some, who see the United States as the evil empire,
view LIC policy as a cover for U.S. imperialism and interventionism.
These people are actively engaged in opposition, actively trying to
organize support against U.S. LIC policy. In a democracy, ideas
prevail not solely because of their rightness, but because of endeavors
of those who hold them. We reach decisions in our society by a
cumbersome, infuriating, damnably slow, and magnificent process of
debate. One cannot succeed without being engaged. This requires
people. People first.

5

The Strategic Imperatives for the United States in Latin America

General Fred F. Woerner

Today's strategic thinking about Latin America is conditioned by views on the prospects for democracy in Central America and in Panama. Yet, we must be careful to avoid becoming mesmerized by recent events in Central America to the exclusion of broader, long-term perspectives on the importance of the entire Latin American region. We need to develop balance in our strategic vision for the Western hemisphere, framed against what Donald E. Nuechterlein calls our four core national interests: homeland defense, economic well-being, international order, and democratic values.[1]

Defining our national interests is challenging. Broad definitions risk identifying all difficulties that arise as threats to the United States that demand an immediate and direct response. The threat, however, may be so indirect and ambiguous that circumspect responses would be more productive. At the same time, narrow definitions of our national interests may obscure real linkages between the political, economic, or social interests and the more obvious military or national security interests. Moreover, narrow definitions, without a clear or overwhelming military threat, may encourage a false sense of well-being. As a result, the kind of visionary and comprehensive planning required to deal with developments before they result in serious or threatening conditions is frequently postponed.

Our core interests are fully engaged in Latin America. Geographic proximity, increasing hemispheric economic interdependence, and common democratic aspirations for an international order free of

This chapter is based on a 1988 Presentation made to a Congressional Subcommittee in support of budget request and subsequently was published by *Military Review* (February 1989), pp. 18–28. It is reprinted here by permission.

violence and military or political dominance by hostile interests all bestow a special importance to the region.

Starting at the beginning of this century with the Panama Canal, U.S. presence and responsibilities have expanded to a regional focus, particularly our support of El Salvador and Honduras and deterrence of Sandinista political and military power, and most recently to support of the democratically elected government of Nicaragua. In doing so, we have committed ourselves to a consistent policy of support for democracy and economic development. As the superpower leader of the world's democratic community, we find out that the measure of our wisdom will be our ability to establish working relationships based on a convergence of our key interests with those of our allies in the region. The central U. S. interest is national security; our allies' interests are independence and dignity.[2] Together, we share a commonality of interests, that include economic and social well-being, and the building of democracy.

The United States depends upon Latin America for its economic health in at least three fundamental ways. First, strategic raw materials such as antimony, manganese, and tin, 96 percent of our bauxite, and 40 percent of our petroleum (to include our entire strategic reserve) come from Latin America. Second, market access for U.S. exports is critical to American jobs; $31.5 billion of U.S. exports went to Latin America in 1987, while we received $44.3 billion in Latin American imports. Third, investment opportunities abound in an area whose population is expected to grow to 549 million by the end of the century. Twenty percent of our total foreign investment and 72 percent of all U.S. investment in the Third World is in Latin America, a region with enormous growth potential.

Immigration and illicit drug traffic are just two of our shared concerns in the area. Illegal immigrants, most of whom come to the United States from Latin America and live on the margins of U.S. society, constitute more than 50 percent of our annual population growth rate. The United States has the fifth largest Spanish-speaking population in the world, now approaching twenty million.

The social consequences of the burgeoning illicit drug trade are well known. Americans consume 60 percent of the world's illegal drugs, and 85 percent of the drugs come from Latin America, and the Caribbean. There are also military and political dimensions to the problem resulting from the increasing linkage between narco-traffickers and insurgent movements. Guerrillas sell protection to narco-traffickers and use the payments to buy military equipment. Vast quantities of drug money are used to suborn governments and corrupt or intimidate military and police forces and judges. The insidious power associated with the world drug trade challenges international order by attacking the core values of a democratic community.

U.S. national defense interests begin with our 1,952 miles of undefended southern border and include the need for access to regional bases. Unfortunately the Soviet Union is virtually on a par with the United States in term of access to land, sea, and air bases in Latin America. Forward-deployed forces include a Soviet brigade and a 2,100-man intelligence center in Cuba. Moreover, access to airfields in Cuba and to the submarine tending base at Cienfuegos poses a threat to democratic interests in the hemisphere.

The Threat to U.S. Strategic Interests

Soviet and Cuban exploitation of endemic economic, political, and social conflict to further their own goals threatens U.S. national interests in Latin America. The internationalization and spread of Marxist insurgencies continue in spite of the remarkable transition to democratically elected governments in the region since 1976. Six nations now have active Marxist insurgencies; three more have incipient ones or suffer spillover effects from neighboring countries. The twenty-five Marxist insurgent groups in Latin America are often supported by the Soviet bloc and Cuba. Until recently, Nicaragua was also a strong supporter of insurgencies. These insurgent groups share a contempt for democratic values. Soviet-surrogate Cuba is well-armed with sophisticated equipment and capable of sustaining global commitments. Soviet aid to Cuba exceeds that given to the rest of the world combined ($16.2 million in economic assistance and $1.7 million in military assistance daily—some $6.3 billion in 1987).

Nicaragua under the Sandinistas represented a national democratic revolution betrayed by a Marxist-Leninist regime committed to the export of revolution. It was committed to supporting the overthrow of democratic governments in neighboring countries and until pressured by the economic disaster within its economy repressed every democratic or anti-Marxist aspect of society. Those activities included the press, the Catholic Church, opposition political forces, the entrepreneurial class, and labor. Moreover, the Sandinista Communist regime imprisoned more opponents of the government than any other nation in the hemisphere except Cuba. It militarized its society with sophisticated conventional weapons to a degree unprecedented in Central American history and unmatched by the collective totals of its four democratic neighbors. Over 50 percent of the national budget was dedicated to the military.

Under the pressure of an economy in full collapse, the lessening of support from the Soviet Union and the call for peace from the other Central American governments, the Sandinistas allowed internationally monitored elections. The results of those elections were a strong repudiation of Sandinista rule and the election of a representative democratic government. The promise for the future of the newest democratic government in Latin America is questionable. The economy is bankrupt after 10 years of Sandinista rule. The Sandinistas still control the military and the instruments of violence within the country. The expectations boosted by the election will not be met without unprecedented outside support. And if the democratic experiment fails, the only forces capable of filling the political vacuum are the Sandinistas.

The spirit of *Perestroika* may lead to the expansion of Soviet-Cuban influence and increasing Soviet presence. Recent evidence of an expanded Soviet role include: reinstatement of diplomatic relations with Cuba by eleven Latin American nations; Soviet diplomatic or economic presence in the thirteen Latin American nations, including high-level visits by Soviet officials; training scholarships to more than 10,000 civilians and military students each year; and trade and technology transfer projects, such as $400 million worth of Soviet agreements with Peru to build fishing and small naval craft.

For emergent Latin American democracies, these events exacerbate the traditional regional problems that historically provide fertile ground for Marxist revolutionaries. Resolving social and economic problems of enormous proportion is fundamental to the security of U.S. interests.

Strategic Imperatives

When referring to the possibility of warfare in Southern Command's theater of operations, I prefer to call it "high probability" instead of low intensity conflict. The first strategic imperative is to build consensus. In doing so, it must be understood that this type of warfare will not be won with technological quick fixes. Rather, the campaign plans are time-intensive and require credible consistency over the long haul. Also, the quick successes to which the American public is attuned and has come to demand as a matter of course will have to give way to progress measured in small increments.

In accomplishing strategic planning for Latin America, the imperatives demand that we focus on support for the democratic process, professionalization of host nation militaries, and legitimization of their role in democratic processes.

At the national level, the United States faces the dilemma of trying to plan military capabilities in light of the risk and intensity of conflict ranging from terrorism, paramilitary narco-guerrillas, and insurgencies to a conventional war or even a strategic nuclear exchange in a NATO setting. As a nation, we are certain to be involved at the mid-to low intensity end of this spectrum. Yet, it is imperative that we respond to the most fundamental of our responsibilities—to guarantee the survival of our way of life. In doing this, we prepare for conflict that most threatens our survivability and make major resource investments for that which is least likely to occur.

Abrams tanks, B-1 bombers, and cruise missiles have little utility in the low intensity/ high probability environment that characterizes the western hemisphere. At the low end of the conflict spectrum, the set of relevant deterrent force options is far more likely to consist of activities encompassing security assistance, combined training exercises, civic action, psychological operations, engineering construction, medical exercises, and infrastructure development.

We must be prepared to apply deterrence theory along the entire spectrum of conflict. The sooner we apply deterrence against threats to U.S. national interests, the lower the ultimate cost will be and the greater will be the range of low-cost options available for countering the threats.

The SOUTHCOM Mission

The mission of U.S. Southern Command is to defend the Panama Canal and the southern flank of the United States and advance U.S. national interests in Latin America. From this flow six specific tasks:

- Maintain the security of the Canal and its southern approaches to the United States.
- Support counterinsurgency operations in El Salvador and help other Latin American militaries combat insurgency, terrorism, and narcotics trafficking.
- Reverse Soviet, Cuban, and Nicaraguan influence and their attempts to destabilize the democratic process in Latin America.
- Plan for contingencies in the theater and be prepared to conduct operations in consonance with U.S. interests.
- Advance U.S. foreign policy objectives.
- Enhance U.S. military influence in the theater and strengthen cohesion with and among our allies.
- To accomplish these aims, force capability requirements are uniquely different from the other unified commands.

SOUTHCOM's theater-based forces include a light infantry brigade, a Special Forces battalion, half a squadron of close-air-support aircraft and a naval special boat unit of nine boats. The most effective force capabilities, however, are not related to the direct application of military power, but rather are more subtle politico-military methods that demonstrate and reinforce the armed forces' legitimate role in a democracy.

Armed forces in democratic societies must be committed to high standards of military professionalism and ethics, supportive of democratic development, respectful of human rights, and subordinate to elected civilian authority.

To acquire the most effective force capabilities, more security assistance is required. This in turn will provide the ability to apply additional force options. Much depends on when we enter the conflict. If we enter the process once armed conflict has already broken out—as we did in El Salvador—the cost is high. If we get involved early, our commitment alone may enable host countries to protect themselves against armed violence, and our long-term cost stands a chance of being less. We have the capability to provide a full range of options at an affordable price. It is important to develop tailored force packages early enough to avoid the undesirable choice of armed intervention at higher cost or acquiescence to a setback to national interests.

Application of the Strategy

The salient points in the application of this strategy are democracy, economic development, and security. Albeit fragile, a process of democratization is taking root in Latin America. In the 1970s, unpopular military governments and dictatorships were the rule. Today, with the exception of Haiti, Panama, and Paraguay, military governments are being replaced by freely elected civilian governments. Since the 5 October 1988 plebiscite, Chile is moving back to the democratic community of nations. At the same time, totalitarian dictatorships dominate Cuba and Nicaragua.

The consolidation of democracy has been a keystore of U.S. policy; another round of dictatorship of the right or left would not advance our national interests. We no longer see an incompatibility between our ideals and our strategic interests. We firmly believe that:

• Democratization in Latin America secures our southern flank and is the best defense against totalitarian inroads.

- Societies that fully engage the creative capacity of their citizens and that hold the governors accountable to the governed contribute more to their and to our national security than do authoritarian governments whose previous claim to legitimacy was their promise of security or their anti-Communist stance.
- Democratic governments are less likely to threaten their people or their neighbors.
- Dictatorships, civilian or military, provide fertile ground for Marxist-Leninist revolutionaries by weakening civilian leadership and, in many cases, corrupting the very guardian of security—a nation's armed forces.

Despite hopeful signs in the democratization process, there has not been a commensurate growth or development in the economic sector. Latin American civilian and military leaders tell us that political democracy cannot long endure without the supporting economic and social development. Distressing signs in this area include declining terms of trade, high unemployment, inflation, declining income levels, inadequate education, virtual decapitalization of some countries because of the foreign debt burden, lack of investor confidence, and inability to generate economic growth.

The male workforce in Mexico now totals 27 million. This figure is projected to grow to 43 million by the turn of the century—and the phenomenal growth rate does not even consider women in, or entering, the labor force. Mexico will have to produce at least one million jobs a year and maintain an 8 percent gross national product (GNP) growth rate for the rest of the century just to keep even with its current unemployment rate. Under the best of circumstances, this is a difficult if not impossible challenge.

The international debt burden across Latin America, which exceeds $410 billion, is so overwhelming that many countries are hard pressed to meet debt servicing requirements and are threatening not to pay or to limit their payments to a percentage of their GNP. This trend discourages additional foreign investment at the very time these nations need $25 billion per year in new investment to achieve 4 to 5 percent real growth in gross domestic product. Latin American governments have paid out more in the last five years to service external debts than they took in during the previous twenty years. Since 1981, the resulting economic austerity has cost the United States $75 billion in lost exports. The progressive "pauperization" of the lower classes in Latin America is a source of dramatic concern to the renascent democracies.

An Action Agenda

Programs to implement the SOUTHCOM strategy are neither exotic nor resource-intensive. Unfortunately, they do not enjoy broad-based civilian or military service constituencies as do many large procurement programs. They are important symbols, however, of long-term commitment to our allies. Failure to fund these force options (less than 3 percent of the Security Assistance budget and one tenth of 1 percent of the Department of Defense budget) will bankrupt the strategy.

The security assistance program assumes greater importance, given the complex threat to our national interests, the lack of sizable deployed force, and the absence of frequent large scale combined military exercises or well-developed alliance structures. Serious impediments in the law make the implementation of a coherent security assistance strategy difficult. These legislative restraints reduce the effectiveness of the security assistance program—restrictions that affect 80 percent of the SOUTHCOM area of responsibility and 71 percent of its population. Lack of multiyear funding needlessly complicates long-term planning. Prohibitions against the use of military assistance for training police and other law enforcement personnel (even though exemptions are permitted by U.S. law) deny interaction with those who most often bear the brunt of defeating well-armed insurgents, terrorists, urban guerrillas, and drug dealers.

Added to these legislative and administrative restrictions is the prospect of greatly diminished funding ceilings in an era of severe budget constraints. Of particular concern are the greatly reduced levels of military assistance programs for El Salvador and Honduras, and the complete elimination of support for all the other Latin American nations except Guatemala and certain countries identified with the illicit drug problem. Continued support for other countries is needed to ensure that the military remains the guarantor rather than arbiter of the democratic process.

If we fail to keep our foot in the door and to provide the bona fides for establishing military-to-military relationships, we forfeit the opportunity for democratic development of other nations. U.S. sanctions, administrative barriers, and low funding ceilings have already opened the door to Soviet, French, British, Chinese, and Israeli arms sales. With these developments came the loss of opportunities for American access, communication, influence, and commerce. Equally disturbing, we are creating a successor generation of

Latin American officers who will have no meaningful U.S. experience as they assume positions of authority. We run the risk of their indifference, if not hostility to U.S. concerns.

Concerning the mobility force option, we are constrained in our access to most of SOUTHCOM's geographic area of responsibility. There are 10,000 airfields in Latin America, but only 500 of them are usable by C-130 aircraft. The requirement for a short take-off and landing aircraft is manifest.

There are 35,000 miles of coastline and more than 50,000 miles of inland waterways in the region that are marginally accessible to our current naval force capabilities. Navy Special Warfare Units, equipped with properly sized patrol craft, provide the basic mobility for us to assist, train, and operate with host nation navy and coastal defense forces. Without sufficient increases in this in-theater naval capability, with which to work with Latin America navies, we will lose an opportunity for professional development of major importance to the overall strategy.

Intelligence is the bedrock of our efforts in the low intensity/high probability conflict environment. We depend on near real-time intelligence with key Latin American countries. This force option remains critical to our agenda.

Force presence, through forward stationing in Panama and exercises, serves to deter Cuban-Nicaraguan aggression and to reassure our democratic allies in the region. Having these theater resources available permits us to train with host nation forces for the type of warfare most likely to be encountered. Exercises and service-funded deployments for training from all four services—often engineer and medical units—are our primary means for achieving a constructive force presence throughout the SOUTHCOM area of responsibility. These JCS exercises and deployments for training are at times our only effective medium for working with host nation militaries. In the past year the Army component of SOUTHCOM, US Army South, alone conducted approximately 300 deployments.

A recent DOD-SOUTHCOM initiative to expand the impact of exercises and deployments for training is the fund for humanitarian and civic assistance under Title 10 of the U.S. Code. This program provides money to support civic action in conjunction with U.S. military activity in the region. The program is coordinated with the Department of State and focuses U.S. military activity to support the concept of democratic legitimacy. In view of scarce or absent security assistance funds, humanitarian and civic assistance can be a powerful supplement to our efforts.

Conclusion

Our national strategy is appropriate. Its effectiveness hinges on a consistent, long-term U.S. commitment, as recommended by the National Bipartisan Commission on Central America in 1984 and reiterated frequently by our national leaders.

We cannot avoid taking sides in this strategic conflict and must remain willing to stand by our neighbors and fellow democracies at a time when they most need our help. We must have the courage to pay the price for as long as it takes. If our enemies become convinced they can wait us out, then no amount of short-term effort will work, and our strategy for the region will be undermined.

Balance in our strategy is equally important. For the past six years, we have been justifiably focused on the security problems of Central America. This center of interest has inevitably slowed the restoration of a security relationship with South America. Our long-term national interests require us to avoid estrangement, loss of political influence, and ultimately, strategic misperceptions in the region.

Protection of U.S. national interests, democratization, and independence of hemispheric nations require a balanced response. We must allocate our efforts between Central and South America and pay attention to big and small nations alike. After carefully assessing the full scope and impact of Soviet-Cuban conventional military power that underwrites Marxist-Leninist insurgent groups in the hemisphere, we must effectively apply the elements of national power to protect our interests.

Although more subtle, the threats to our national security interests in Latin America are every bit as real as those posed by the Warsaw Pact in Europe. Moreover, we do not have 40 years of orderly development in our strategic thought about how to deal with these gray areas of threat, nor have we applied in consistent fashion our strategy of deterrence and flexible response to the low intensity/high probability conflict environments in the Third World. We must view these threats for what they are and underwrite the conditions that will allow the fragile Latin American democracies to mature. Moreover, we must persuade those nations with dictatorships of the right or left to grant to their people the right of choice.

The preamble to the Central American Peace Accords, agreed to by five Central American presidents in 1987, states that "peace and development are indivisible." An unstated, but obvious, corollary for American foreign and national security policy is that peace and freedom are inseparable.

It is time that we take full measure of our national interests in Latin

America. A strategy without resources is empty rhetoric that leads to failure and frustration. The fundamental question is our willingness to step in with an enduring commitment to democracy and economic development in this hemisphere and to underwrite the relatively low costs of providing the security shield behind which they can be achieved.

Notes

1. Donald F. Nuechterlein, *America Overcommitted: United States National Interests in the 1980s*, (Lexington: University of Kentucky Press, 1985).

2. David Ronfeldt, *Geopolitics, Security and U. S. Strategy in the Caribbean Basin*, (Santa Monica: Rand Corporation, 1987).

6

The Umbrella of Legitimacy

Courtney E. Prisk

Success in a counterinsurgency, as in all uncomfortable wars, is predicated on the ability of a government to understand the total phenomena involved. An essential error of many embattled regimes fighting for survival is the failure to realize that the central goal of an insurgency is not to defeat the armed forces, but to subvert or destroy the government's legitimacy, its ability and its moral right to govern.

If the multidimensional nature of the threats in an uncomfortable war were understood, a government and its allies would develop strategies to enhance or maintain both political and moral legitimacy as well as to combat effectively the insurgent armed forces. Numerous studies since the late 1950s have highlighted the indirect nature of the threats and the criticality of the legitimacy dimension.[1] These studies show that the United States is replete with rhetorical understanding of the fundamental requirement for legitimacy. Yet, when engaged, the energy, resources, and attention of the United States are continually and almost exclusively focused on the tactics of fighting the opposing armed forces.[2]

A similar focus led to a basically one-dimensional military response to the multidimensional threats faced in Algeria in the 1950s, in Vietnam in the 1960s, and in Peru in the 1980s. In each, the failure to understand and to develop strategies and capabilities to protect and enhance the moral underpinnings of the government in power, in Clausewitzian terms the principal "center of gravity" target, ensured that the insurgents maintained the psychological advantage and political offensive.[3]

Legitimacy—The Insurgent's Target

Often individuals of one nation will question the legitimacy of another based on fundamental differences in political philosophy. Notwithstanding the type of political philosophy that guides a country, however, on the international stage the necessities of international affairs assume the legitimacy of government in power until there is serious debate or struggle within the country. Regardless of the type of government, the test of legitimacy is first the purview of the governed. If there is a tranquil acceptance or nationwide majority support and minority acceptance, the method of governance is assumed to be politically legitimate both nationally and internationally. If, however, there is internal strife created by real or perceived social or economic injustices, or if there is internal conflict created by discontented elites or external forces, the legitimacy of the incumbent government becomes the subject of open debate and even insurgent warfare.

An understanding that political philosophies and legitimacy vary with the social and historical background of a country is crucial to the ability to measure a government's internal strength. In the simplest terms, varying political philosophies somehow propose balancing equality and individual freedoms while maintaining the government's ability to provide physical protection and economic viability for the nation. A U.S. or Western observer attempting to assess and prescribe the best for a government or a people often fails to understand that his perception of freedom, equality, or economic viability may differ significantly from the perceptions of those directly involved. Recognizing this essential difference in perceptions is central to the capability of assessing and developing strategies for an embattled government to maintain and enhance legitimacy.

The second component of this essential difference in perceptions is the political philosophy of the principal outside power(s) supporting the government or the insurgent. Here, if the regime seeking support fails to understand the perceptions of moral legitimacy, that are basic to the supporting power's political system, the regime will limit the ability of that outside power to continue to provide assistance.

What does political philosophy have to do with warfare and counterinsurgencies? The simple answer is everything. The primary center of gravity for the insurgents' attack on the government is the political legitimacy of the government in power. The very heart of an insurgency is the challenge against the incumbent's moral right to govern. The basis for this challenge is rooted in the belief that the current government system is not providing, and cannot or will not provide, the necessary balance between equality, freedom, and security for the people, and that the challenger's political philosophy and system are the truly representative method that will provide that balance.

A regime faced with an uncomfortable war must by the nature of that war concentrate first on its political legitimacy by continuing to demonstrate the ability to govern. However, failure to understand the basic threat as an attack not only on the structures of the government and the economic infrastructure of society—the most obvious overt targets—but also on the very basic moral right to govern means that the regime is doomed to eventual defeat.

During the remainder of this chapter, the terms moral and political legitimacy will be used.[4] For some, there is a semantic battle between the two. While they are closely linked, there is a distinction because of the multiple actors in an insurgency. Political legitimacy is an internal dynamic referring to the support given to a regime by the populace and the social institutions within a country. It is based on cultural and historical factors and can be measured in terms of the political philosophy and the degree to which a government is able to meet the social and economic needs of a country. There is a moral component to political legitimacy in terms of the means by which the government abides and does not violate the cultural norms of the society, but political legitimacy deals most specifically with the government's ability to govern internally.

Moral legitimacy is both an internal and an external dynamic. It is based on judgment of the methods by which the government or insurgents apply their power to achieve their ends. The very existence of an insurgency is an indication that certain portions of the populace challenge that moral legitimacy has been lost or forfeited. The *Proceso de Reorganizacion Nacional* that ruled Argentina from 1976 to 1983 was infamous for its brutality and systematic use of state terror.[5] Despite the growing evidence of repression and morally reprehensible use of force, however, it was not until the debacle over the Falklands/Malvinas that the Argentine civil society and institutions withdrew their support, and the political legitimacy of the military government was lost.[6]

Moral legitimacy of a government or an insurgency becomes very important externally as a component in the success or failure of an insurgency. The application of standards of acceptable moral behavior as a prerequisite for external support is very much a function of the provider's political philosophy and purpose. Being anti-capitalistic or pro-Soviet may be the only constraints the Soviets rigidly impose on their support for a government or an insurgent movement. The Soviet philosophy and doctrine include the destruction of the existing society and advocate violent and extralegal means to attain the goals of instituting state socialism.[7]

Built into the Marxist-Leninist philosophy is the notion that all means justify the communist end. As such, elimination or neutralization of anyone and everything opposing that ultimate end can be rationalized. If their cause is advanced and supported, the Soviets' moral considerations for providing aid to a government or insurgency appear to be of little consequence. This is a very convenient philosophy for insurgents to adopt. By declaring Marxist-Leninist philosophy and goals, the insurgents can garner outside support, while at the same time pursuing all means from propaganda to terrorism to drug trafficking to total destruction of the society to accomplish their goals.

However, in those situations in which the United States is providing the external support, moral legitimacy acts as "a single-edged knife that cuts only into the American body politic and leaves the Soviet leadership (and surrogate supporters of the insurgents) unscathed."[8] Moral legitimacy is a constraint that has a selective and somewhat one-sided impact on the participants in a conflict. This is especially true for the United States in the 1990s. One of of the most important dimensions for success in an uncomfortable war is the strength, commitment, and consistency of external support.[9] More and more, the determinant of U.S. ability to have a strong and consistent commitment is the perception of moral legitimacy by the U.S. body politic.

U.S. policy/decision makers have failed to build consensus and an understanding of the need for patience in light of our constraints. This failure points to still another critical aspect to understanding the battles of the war for legitimacy. We need to understand that the perception of legitimacy is different in societies without the same traditions or experiences as the United States and that "democracy," though having certain basic common elements, has many forms. While many U.S. policy/decision makers perceive that achieving legitimacy through pluralistic and distributive power is the correct method, one of the major problems in Latin America (and most Third World nations) is amassing enough central capability to deal with the various dimensions of the conflict.[10]

In Latin America, traditional political societies and governing elites face a period of forced transition. For the most part, these countries have imbedded in their constitutions the principles of authoritarian rule as the basis for that nation's political legitimacy.[11] These principles included centralization of authority, hierarchical rule through administrative (nonparliamentary) agencies at provincial and local levels, and a "flexible" constitution that has offered little effective constraint on the exercise of governmental authority.[12] Attempts to meet the needs of the people and the social structures have tended toward granting or extending political participation in a manner that integrates competing power centers, discourages the development of strong opposition parties, preserves existing privileges, and maintains the basic authoritarian tenets. Today, with accelerating changes, the increasing difference between population growth and economic growth, rising expectations, and increased global communications, the traditional structures and governing elite no longer have the luxury (or the power) to contemplate moderate change. The option of accommodating competing interests within the traditional authoritarian structure is no longer viable, and dramatic or revolutionary change appears to be the future for most countries in the region.

Indicators of Legitimacy

What, then, are the measures of political and moral legitimacy in Latin America? What impact do these factors have on the five major actors in an uncomfortable war? General Galvin in chapter 1 identifies the three principals in an insurgency as the government, the guerrillas, and the people. To this we need to add two additional actors, the countries providing external support to each of the opposing combatants. The weight and impact given to specific indicators will vary from significant to meaningless depending on the objectives of the particular actor.

Taking into account the government, the people, and external support by the U.S. government, there are at least five conditional indicators of legitimacy that apply to the region: (1) Free and fair election; (2) political participation on the part of the populace; (3) the government's ability to extract and distribute resources; (4) active or tacit approval of the social institutions; (5) a fair and just judicial system. Although we discuss each indicator separately, in reality they are interwoven. To an acceptable degree, all of these indicators must be operative and positive for a government to win the legitimacy dimension of an uncomfortable war.

Free, Fair, and Frequent Elections

Free elections, as a measure, mean the absence of corruption, intimidation, and fear in the political process. If a significant portion of a populace votes in an environment free of coercion, this is a strong indicator that the winning government or party is assumed to be legitimate.

Free and fair elections have, as a measure, several inherent assumptions. First, inherent in the idea of being fair is the existence of a viable opposition. Equally inherent is the underlying acceptance that, whoever the winners, they will be allowed to govern. In a democracy, the results of a free and fair election resolve the issue of who should succeed as the leaders of the government. As basic as these ideas may appear, the suppression, assimilation, or active elimination of opposing views—in the name of unity—has been one of the traditionally accepted precepts of Latin American politics for about as long as the United States has practiced universal suffrage.[13] In many Latin American countries an alternate precept exists which, although not as strong, stresses the importance of developing a viable opposition. Still, tolerance of political conflict and opposition historically wanes in times of economic or political crisis.[14]

The difference between the political challengers or competing power centers in a developed Western democracy and those challengers in developing countries is that in a developed Western democracy, the opposition can prevail through the ballot box. As Glen C. Dealy stated in his article on "The Pluralistic Latins," "For 150 years Latin American governments have endeavored not to balance competing centers of power, but either to integrate or to eliminate them in the name of collective harmony."[15] The desired balance point on the spectrum of freedoms in Latin America has periodically shifted back and forth, especially during periods of reform. However, taking a view over several time periods, the trend has favored order and unity, opting for more structure, centralized control, and harmony.

The fostering of free and fair elections within a society unfamiliar with the ideas of pluralistic democracy and under the stress of attempting to fight an ongoing insurgency is not easy. In El Salvador, as an example, the successful implementation of elections (1982, 1984, 1985, 1988 and 1989) has been heralded as a significant historical event. What was enlightening about the 1982 elections, which saw 80 percent of the people vote despite serious threats from the insurgents, is that President Alvaro Magana, at the age of 55, voted for the first time.[16] It was not because there had been no previous elections, but because up to that time, he had seen no point in voting. This was even true in 1972, when the Christian Democratic Party, under Jose Napoleon Duarte, was sufficiently strong to provide a viable alternative to the military party.

Perhaps more enlightening are the comments by former President Duarte that "democracy cannot exist without a viable opposition and without an opposition there is no democracy."[17] As elemental as this may sound, the whole concept of a "loyal opposition" is fundamentally alien to countries that have for centuries accepted Rousseau's premise that unanimity and harmony are the basic ingredients of community.[18] Opposition elements tend to disrupt unity and public order and, as such, are to be integrated if they are powerful, or suppressed/ eliminated if weak in order to "ensure domestic tranquility."[19]

For a government seeking to build consensus and sufficient power to get something done, the fostering of increased pluralism and a viable opposition means opening the door to the increased inefficiency of democratic governance. It means that the regime must move away from the traditional societal desire for unanimity toward a point allowing greater personal freedom and criticism of the government. This is a fundamental shift for many Latin Americans, and it is not an obvious, intuitively desired shift for all the institutions and societies of this region. Nevertheless, it is required by the newly created expectations of the "people." In terms of the Western world, especially the United States, viable opposition is important as a major real and symbolic aspect of democracy.

Participation

While the presence of a constitutional framework and the occurrence of periodic elections are important measures, they should not be considered by themselves as sufficient indicators of legitimacy. All political systems limit participation. Whether acceptable or not to outside cultures and societies, the philosophical basis for limiting participation in a specific country is usually rooted in longstanding, traditional concepts—most of which can be found in a constitution. The constitutions of many Latin American countries, especially those of Central America, were rewritten in the early and late nineteenth century to conform closely to the U.S Constitution of 1787.[20] The chief difference in the application of the framework was that in practice, the powers of the chief executives in Latin America were far greater, and the abilities of the legislative and judicial branches to act independently were limited.[21]

There has been notable liberalization of the political processes in most Latin American countries over the past decade. The number and trend of Latin American dictatorships that have begun the liberalization processes that could lead to democracy are often cited.[22] However, to assess the strength of political or moral legitimacy, in terms of a country's ability to counteract and defeat an insurgency, it is necessary to look at the context in which the liberalization has taken place and the extent to which the populace participates in the political process.

The key to legitimacy for a particular method of governance is the acceptance and support by an adequate percentage of the people, including nonparticipants in the political power sharing. Traditionally, Latin America has been steeped in strong centralized government in the Napoleonic (Rousseauistic) tradition.[23] The New England concepts of a local town government self-governing in limited areas prescribed by county, state, or federal authorities is not a model that easily fits most countries in Latin America.[24] Local and provincial leaders and administrators in Latin America draw their authority from the central government, but traditionally apply the rules in a rather autonomous manner.[25] Participation in the traditional sense meant voting or supporting the local patrons who, in turn, provided the benefits and services. Quite often, the more the support, the more the benefits. [26] On the other hand, the less the support the greater the depression.

The introduction of mass media communication has tended to erode tacit acceptance of the traditional systems. As knowledge and understanding of differing life styles have raised the level of expectations, the populace in Latin American countries has begun to demand more and better services. More and more the ability to deliver those services has become the means by which the regime's legitimacy is measured. The ability of the people to influence the delivery of services—as well as the general distribution of desired benefits—by participating in the political process is a prime indicator of the government's political legitimacy. As the expectations of the individuals rise, the capability of the government to foster and to respond to increased participation becomes a significant measure of a regime's ability to govern.

Probably equally important as the perceived ability to influence the delivery of basic services is the concept recognized in the government's political process that the individual will have protection for his family and property and the ability to influence the redress of inequities and social grievances (through either individual or institutional means). Again, as basic as these ideas may appear, in Latin America (without a history of limited and nationally responsive local government or viable political opposition) the ability to influence the decisions of a central government through individual participation is a concept not easily accepted or implemented. [27]

For centuries, the individual Latin American has participated by/through association with a societal institution—the Church, the Army, the bureaucracy, the labor union, the corporate entity, or the political party with which he is associated.[28] What was good for those entities was assumed by the societies to be the best for the individual. Glen Dealy refers to this type of Latin American democracy as "social" or "economic" democracy in which there is "a government of or for but not necessarily by the people."[29] As demands for more equity, better benefits, and more services increase in Latin America, the need to reform or restructure the means of participating in and influencing the government becomes a primary, first-level requirement of legitimacy.

For the United States, the perception that there is a viable way in which the individual can and does participate in the political processes of a nation is extremely important. In order to provide strong, consistent support, U.S. policy/decision-makers must build consensus and support not only for the allied regime, but also for the "people" of that nation. Here the concepts of individual participation and government accountability are ingrained in the U.S. and Western political philosophy as the symbolic measure of democracy.

Ability to Extract and Distribute Resources

The primary means of a government to enforce policy or ensure services is through the extractive and distributive mechanisms of the society. There are three traditional areas in which the extraction of resources is important: treasure, time, and blood. Strong measures of a regime's legitimacy are its ability to gain voluntary services and its ability to fill the ranks of its armed forces.

For both the regime in power and the U.S. support for that regime, the ability to provide resources for the government becomes an absolute requirement and a measurement of legitimacy. In the Western democratic view, the inability to extract sufficient resources without resorting to coercion is considered a sign that the people do not support the government and, as a negative measure of political legitimacy.

Of interesting note, a government's ability to solicit outside economic support to overcome internal problems often is perceived as a positive sign of legitimacy. Cuba's experience shows that its government cannot generate sufficient internal economic means to support the country. However, because the Cuban government can maintain its capability to provide for the minimum requirements of the people through daily infusion of funds from the Soviet Union, the government is considered by the populace as politically legitimate. No mention of the repressive nature of the Cuban government is needed except to note that a country that wants the support of the United

States must move more and more away from repression and toward
legitimacy in the sense of human rights and persuasion.

As a government moves away from coercion and attempts to govern
through increased cooperation and the generation of individual
responsibility, the measure of legitimacy for the people becomes
how well the government is able to provide or distribute basic services
and protection for the people.[30] For a government attempting to
reflect pluralistic values there is a dual test of how well it performs
the responsibilities of governance and how well it matches the
values and needs of the people who support it.[31] If a government
is competent yet hostile to the needs of the people, or amenable
but incompetent, selective, or corrupt in its delivery of services, it
tends to forfeit its legitimacy.[32] The fall of the Marcos The
government in the Philippines is a case in point. The incompetent
handling of the economy and the corruption of the "crony socialism"
rendered that regime incapable of meeting the needs of the
people.[33]

Maintaining competence in the delivery of services while attempting to fight an insurgency is no easy task. Faced with an enemy who
deliberately attacks the government's competence by destroying power
lines, transportation means and other basic services, that government
is hard pressed simply to maintain or repair existing services. A
military critic may allude to such insurgent actions against government
delivery of services as "fighting-on-the-cheap". The fact of the
matter is that insurgent destruction of basic services and insurgent
repression of the people strike at the Clausewitzian "center of
gravity—in this case, the government's legitimacy. [34]

Active or Tacit Approval of Social Institutions

As difficult as extraction or distribution of resources is during
periods of insurgency or after a disaster such as an earthquake, the
gaining and maintaining of tacit or active support from major societal
institutions may be even more demanding. The basic problems of a
society in transition cannot be solved by the central government acting
alone. This effort requires the cooperation of business, unions,
educational institutions, local governments, and, particularly in Latin
America, the Church and the military.

The active or tacit approval and cooperation of societal institutions
are a double-edged sword. Each institution has a different agenda, a
different set of interests. These interests usually center around the four
"great themes of political argument". These themes are liberty,
equality, efficiency, and quality of life.[35] The agendas of the

politically powerful institutions in a country will tend toward one of the poles established by the four themes.

While couching constitutional rhetoric in terms of unity and equality, the authoritarian oligarchic regimes of Latin America have tended almost exclusively toward the pole of efficiently maintaining the economic structure and social largesse beneficial to the controlling and emerging elites. The traditional societal structure, including the Church and the military along with the oligarchy, has benefited the most by maintaining ordered efficiency. The combination of nineteenth-century economic liberalism and corporate oligarchic structure continued to promote the interests of the ruling power centers.[36]

In terms of the people, the impact of mass communications, the rise of liberation theology, and the active export of Marxist-Leninist labor philosophy have radically changed the roles of the social institutions in Latin America.[37] There is now more clamoring for true political freedoms, and for more egalitarian distribution of income and wealth, and a struggle for a concept of how to achieve these goals. In a country struggling to fight an insurgency, the government's political legitimacy is measured by its ability to create policies that gain the support of major institutions while meeting the challenges posed by the situation and the needs of the people. With a strong history of political participation through institutions, Latin American governments must alter the political roles of the institutions without alienating the power elite within them.

A government can no longer be perceived as ruling merely for the benefit of a single class, as was the case in El Salvador prior to 1979.[38]

Neither can a regime operate in a manner alienating a major social sector, as did Marcos with the business community in the Philippines.[39] Nor can the government ignore and repress sectors of the population, like the Indians in Guatemala and Peru.[40] Moreover, the elite cannot rule for the benefit of one institution over another as did the Argentine military.[41]

In order to maintain or enhance legitimacy with the people, governments must extend their writ to all social groups and seek active support not only for the regime in power but for the entire system. The growing focus of change in the Third World is on increased satisfaction of social needs.[42] The goal of efficiency can no longer be the principal concern. While the underlying desire for unity will remain a powerful force in Latin American systems, the political and moral legitimacy of their governments will more and more be measured upon their ability to balance the competing values within the entire system, incorporating the needs for social-economic justice and the interests of the major social institutions.

In this changing environment, the importance of developing consensus for real change toward redress of the root economic and social causes of conflict cannot be overstated. In order to build that consensus, and to maintain political legitimacy, the regime in power must seek a type of change that allows the social institutions of the country to change and internalize new concepts of behavior and responsibility. The alternative would be a collapse of the institutions and subsequent total destruction of the society. As with the situation in Argentina after the Falkland/Malvinas defeat, if a government loses the support of the principal institutions in the society, it also loses the means of maintaining legitimacy within that society.[43]

Critical to successfully building external and internal consensus for change are two institutions within the Latin American countries that have both a trained body of administrators and a nationwide organization—the Church and the military.

The Church

As one of the most pervasive and historic institutions in Latin America, the Church has "ruled hand-in-glove first with the colonial authorities and later at the side of the power elites in the independent republics that were born in the nineteenth century".[44] The attempts by liberals in the nineteenth and early twentieth century to limit the land holdings, privileges, and powers of the Church tended to strengthen the bonds between it and the authoritarian conservative elements. [45]

Today, when assessing institutional support as a measure of political legitimacy, we need to consider three aspects of the Church's role in Latin American politics. First, for the most part the nations of the region do not have a constitutional separation of church and state.[46] While in most countries it can be argued that there is de facto separation, the Church has an accepted role in supporting and mediating in politics. Second, although the rise of liberation theology is assisting insurgent movements and is tending to modify the Church's stance,[47] the institution and its leadership continue to support the more conservative authoritarian power-centers by continuing to adopt a preservationist posture.[48] Third, the Church has been and remains a major legitimizing institution in the countries of the region. It is a force for political legitimacy and, increasingly for the external component, for moral legitimacy.

The Military

Similar to the Church, the militaries in Latin America have been pervasive elements in the support, sharing, and dominance of political power. Also like the Praetorian guard, the militaries of Latin America (especially since the birth of the independent republics) have often used their power to overthrow the leadership and to control the "election" (selection) of successive leaders.[49]

The regional history of military intervention, and to a great extent the role this institution plays in events of today, must be understood in the context that the military in most Latin American nations is an accepted integral, institutional participant in the political processes. The militaries have for their part internalized the concept or image that they are the leading nationalists. The military officers and leadership see their role as protectors of the constitution, the rights of the people, and the "idealized" system in being. Yet, not uncharacteristically, Latin American officers commonly believe that "politics" is "dissension."[50] And, "more than any other elite group, [these] military officers view political parties as undesirable agents of disunity."[51]

When assessing the institutional role of the military in ensuring a system of peaceful change, the observer or advisor needs to recognize the Latin American military officer's strong bias for the philosophical concepts of unity and harmony. Rooted in centuries of Rousseauistic teachings,[52] the natural tendency of the military leadership is to discourage opposition and those types of political conflict that are inherent in the political party competition within North American and West European democracies.[53] It is necessary, however, especially in the view of the United States, that the modern professional military accept the discord that accompanies the process of democracy.

Dynamic change threatens the "old guard", which tends to protect that environment in which it has thrived.[54] Short of radically revamping the whole institutional structure, significant change in a well established institution, such as the military, will only take place in those situations in which the "old guard" can maintain collective and individual self-esteem.[55] Third World civilian regimes must understand, in this period of forced transition, the need to provide the philosophical bases for the military institution to accommodate change.[56] Knowing that all institutions will fight change that threatens their survival, it is necessary to foster concepts of purpose that encourage and even reward the military establishments to redefine their corporate interests and to adopt changes.

In support of both the regime and the people, one role of the
professional military is to ensure peaceful continuance or succession of
the government and, in its internal defense role, to protect and promote
institutionalized, freely competitive elections and to ensure that a
peaceful continuance or transfer of power takes place based on the
election results.[57] If the military withholds institutional support of a
duly elected government, as in Chile during the Allende regime, or
intimidates the electoral process to falsify the results of an election,
as in El Salvador during the 1972 presidential Election, or in Panama
during the 1984 and 1989 presidential elections the result is a lessening
of both moral and political legitimacy.[58]

Both the government system (immediately) and the military (in
the long term) are weakened by the recurrence of praetorianism. Not
only does militarization of government weaken the civil service, as
was demonstrated in the Philippines over the past two decades, but
disruption of the democratic processes and replacement of civilian
administrative personnel do not allow for the growth of a responsible
civil sector. In addition to the overall weakening of the structure of
government, as is evident in Panama today, concentration of economic
control and the means of violence (military power), in the name of
order and efficiency, leads to corruption and/or repression.

In terms of internal political stability, the intrusion of the military
into the democratic process—abridging or setting aside the legal/
constitutional rules—opens the door to subversive or insurgent groups.
Disregard by the military for the legal processes only serves to build
credibility for insurgent claims against the government and, thereby,
exposes this primary center of gravity to attack.

For the United States, the political role played by the military is
one of main factors that make an insurgency an uncomfortable war.
Allied governments and their military leadership need to recognize
and to understand that, in the perception of the United States, the
only correct role of a professional military is one in which that
institution is subordinate and subservient to the elected civilian
government.

There are countries in which the regime in power has received
continued U.S. support despite abuses of human rights and flagrant
abuses of power by the military. Henry Kissinger suggests that the
realpolitik criterion for this continuing support is based on the higher
moral grounds represented by war and peace. This is especially true in
the East European context and perhaps decreasingly true in the Korean
situation.[59]

In most Third World countries, however, the nature of a country-
specific threat is not so compelling that it raises or engages the U.S.

body politic to be concerned about regional or global war. Indeed, the ability of a country-specific threat to generate concern about even a portion of the United States' overall interests is questionable. It is because of the ambiguous nature of the threat to the United States that issues of moral legitimacy become basic determining factors in uncomfortable wars.

Absent a compelling threat to U.S. interests, recognized by the majority of the U.S. body politic, the willingness and ability of the United States to become involved in uncomfortable wars will become increasingly constrained and selective. In this light, the criterion for involvement will be more and more based on the perceived moral legitimacy of the regime. Perhaps the lesson of Chile and the unwillingness of the United States to support the Pinochet government is a good case in point. Although the United States was fundamentally opposed to the Marxist Allende government, there was no compelling threat to U.S. interests that overshadowed the basic moral issues represented by the military's abuse of power after the overthrow of the elected regime. Nor have the demonstrated economic efficiency and competence of the military rule in Chile over the past decade totally justified, in the U.S. calculus, the repression and subversion of democratic processes.

For the people and the regime of a country, fostering strong, viable, and competitive social institutions strengthens the pluralistic base for political legitimacy. In terms of the United States, the ability of a regime to govern with the active or tacit approval of the major societal institutions, along with its ability to constrain the abuses of power and to hold these institutions accountable, is one of the primary indicators of both political and moral legitimacy.

Fair and Just Judicial System

Perhaps the adage "power corrupts and absolute power corrupts absolutely" is one of the underlying thoughts that should apply to any discussion of legitimacy. Indeed, the extensive study into factors determining the success or failure in an uncomfortable war highlighted that corruption was one of the most pervasive factors in the loss of regime legitimacy.[60] Certainly this was the case in the demise of the Marcos regime in the Philippines and of the Somoza regime in Nicaragua.[61]

Widespread corruption and abuse of power exist because they are tacitly condoned by the major societal institutions and because there are no consistent methods of holding the powerful accountable. The situation in Panama prior to the removal of Noriega, was but one example. In this case the description of the country given to new diplomats and potential new businessmen was to consider Panama more as Tammany Hall and the mob rather than as a sovereign nation. Indeed, much of the discontent in Third World nations centers around the inability or unwillingness of regimes to bring to justice those individuals or groups who obviously flaunt moral or judicial laws. The failure of various countries to bring to justice known members of the military "death squads" or to stop the repression of the Indian minorities by their police forces are but two examples.[62] Somoza abridged the law of his country and had his cronies change the constitution so that he could be elected again.[63] His open misappropriation of earthquake relief funds led to both internal and external discontent and then virtual isolation of his regime, and still he was able to "win" reelection.[64]

There cannot be moral legitimacy if the scales of justice can be manipulated. A judicial system that can be manipulated or bought is the weakest link in any government. In order for a democratic government to be considered legitimate, every person and every institution within that nation must be subordinate to the rule of law— to the rules of the system.[65] As inherently obvious as this idea may seem, in parts of Latin America, and of the world, the judicial systems are in many respects just emerging from the Seventeenth Century. These systems are descended from the Spanish sovereign rule (the divine right of kings) and were set up to protect the interests of, and were dependent upon, the ruling elites or power centers.[66]

For the Third World peoples and governments faced with the current environment in which dynamic or revolutionary forced transition will take place, judicial independence and effectiveness are requirements for lasting and meaningful democratic change. If the justices can be cowed, as in Colombia or the Philippines, or at the mercy of the executive or military, as in Panama or Bolivia, there can be no real The justice or moral legitimacy.[67] When the constitution or laws can be changed at the whim of the ruling regime, minority or opposition rights cannot be guaranteed, and there will exist no effective counter to corruption or the abuses of human and civil rights.

In terms of building consensus within the United States to support an ally, nothing appears more damaging than the failure to curb corruption or abuses of power. In reaction to the abuses of power and the corruption by Somoza, the United States withdrew financial and military assistance even though that meant the likely victory of the Sandinistas.[68] The flagrant open corruption and disregard for human rights in Panama caused the United States to suspend all assistance to the Noriega regime. The perception that Noriega and his regime were neither morally nor politically legitimate built a constraint that impeded the ability of the United States to assist Panama as long as that regime was in power. While Panama was not faced with an insurgency, Panama was and is as important to United States strategic interests as any nation in the region. In this situation there exists a reasonably compelling case for a potential threat to U.S. interests. The lack of U.S. willingness to interact with the Noriega regime, its willingness to withdraw support from the country, and its subsequent attack to remove Noriega and his military supporters should be a signal to all governments that flagrant corruption and abuses of individual rights are moral legitimacy issues which will be determinant factors in future U.S. relations.

Implications for the Future

There are many aspects under the umbrella of legitimacy that must be understood at two distinctly different levels. For the principal actors in current and future uncomfortable wars, political legitimacy must be understood as the primary target not only to be protected, but also to be enhanced in the majority of the situations. Likewise, combatants looking to the United States for assistance and support need to understand that legitimacy, in the perception of the growing majority of the U.S. body politic, is a major moral issue that will constrain US willingness and ability to become effectively involved.

To set preconditions for support of another government is not a new phenomenon in international affairs. In terms of U.S. support, the concept of imposing constraints based on U.S. beliefs concerning moral legitimacy has indeed become a factor that must be included in the calculus.

In dictating preconditions, to include championing human rights, redress of social and economic injustices, and democratic reforms, it is important for U.S. policy-makers to understand that the perception of political legitimacy varies greatly in societies built on different political backgrounds and experiences. Likewise, it is important to understand that it is counterproductive in the long term to require a developing nation, facing an insurgency, to attempt to demonstrate immediately the ability to apply refined forms, procedures, and ideals of the U.S. government model.

An embattled government that lacks a pluralistic tradition or sufficient trained administrators and attempts to implement a mature democracy fosters unattainable expectations. In turn, failure to meet these expectations gives the insurgents increased credibility, gives them fuel for their propaganda war against the government, and lessens the internal perception of the regime's political legitimacy. Failure on the part of U.S. policy/decision makers to appreciate the impact of imposing upon a developing democracy a strict requirement to implement the U.S style of government only reinforces the suggestion that "American proficiency at imparting technical skills is matched only by American insensitivity to local conditions.[69]

It is important for all observers to note that while Marxism has been and will continue to be a crucial element in Third World politics, in Latin America (and in Central America particularly) traditional Catholicism and conservatism have leaned toward growing anti-communist and pro-democratic sentiments since the Sandinistas took power in 1979.[70] These growing sentiments, along with erosion of tacit acceptance of traditional oligarchic systems, are the forces bringing regional leaders, such as former President Duarte, to the conclusion that there must be either a democratic revolution or a totalitarian socialist revolution.[71] Since the totalitarian socialist utopia requires total unity and submission to the central will, it is simply impossible to achieve in a society where there are differing values, and the efforts and direction must be toward a legitimate democracy—a democracy founded on a fair and just rule of law, one seeking to balance competing institutional values on the basis of justice.

When totalitarian prescriptions for change threaten the very concepts of personal freedom and liberty, support of democracy is a viable strategy for the United States in the world. Today many governments and people seek to cope with the forced transitions from authoritarian philosophies to one based on a political and moral legitimacy. In this milieu, not only does the United States need to provide the tools to fight against something such as an insurgent armed force, but also it must begin to develop, through new and innovative legislation and understanding, the means to fight for something—to assist embattled countries to establish lasting capabilities to strengthen both political and moral legitimacy.

Beyond the fostering of a just and fair legal system, that assistance is essential for all measures. It must assist in the essential ability of a government to extract and distribute the treasure and services of the country in an impartial, fair, and equitable manner. The assistance should not hinge on agreement with a particular policy or administration. What should be required, however, is that the implementation of policy and programs not be perceived as either arbitrary or contrary to the public good or to individual freedoms. The rules for extracting or implementing public services need to be clearly articulated (within cultural norms), based on participatory input (widely understood), and perceived as fair.

For their part, Third World regimes must understand that support from the United States will not be forthcoming unless the "American body politic" perceives the direction of the changes to be both morally and politically legitimate.[72] There is an ongoing process of change within the U.S. body politic concerning support for Third World regimes. As this change is taking place, there is also a different sense of the threat to American values and standards of living that is continuing to develop. While realistic options and accommodations will remain available to U.S. decision/policy makers for short-term action or reaction, in the long term, especially in those areas where the threats to U.S. interests are indirect or ambiguous, moral concerns for social justice and equity will increasingly become the constraints dictating the ability to provide assistance. While the touchstone of political stability was satisfactory for the realpolitik of the past, today it is not enough. In the arena of the uncomfortable war, it has become obvious that political and moral legitimacy, not simply political stability, are required to solve the root causes of the conflicts and to manage the forced transition.

Equally obvious for the foreseeable future, the ability of the United States to assist a regime or government will be predicated on and directly related to the perception of moral legitimacy on the part of that government by U.S. policy makers and the American public.

Notes

1. In 1959, the Draper Commission report concluded that the United States needed to understand the indirect nature of the threats and the political constraints of the host nation military. The Howze Board in 1962 recommended significant increases in training for all aspects of counterinsurgency. The Defense Science Board, under Dr. Harold Brown, reported in 1964 that training and organization must stress the social science nature of the "limited war" the United States was likely to face. National Security Action Memorandum (NSAM) 182, published in August 1962, was specific in directing that U.S. strategy should support the building of internal defense in such a manner as to ameliorate the root social and political causes. In March 1963, the U.S. Army published its concept for Special Action Forces (SAF); a major tenet of the SAF was to "use police, intelligence, civic action, and psychological operations to ameliorate root causes of insurgency". The Army's Low Intensity Conflict Project Final Report of August 1986 pointed out at "as a nation we do not understand low intensity conflict," including the fundamental aspect of legitimacy. The *Model for Analysis of Insurgencies*, originally researched at the Army War College and published in February 1987 by the Small Wars Operations Research Directorate, United States Southern Command,

concluded that the "legitimacy dimension" was the most critical of the seven dimensions.

2. Sir Robert Thompson, "Defeating Communist Insurgency; The Lesson of Malaya and Vietnam," *Studies In International Security*, 10 (New York: Frederick A. Praeger, 1967), p. 51.

3. Sam C. Sarkesian, "Low Intensity Conflict: Concepts, Principles, and Policy Guidelines," *Air University Press* (January–February 1985), p. 8.

4. John T. Fishel and Edmund S. Cowan provide an excellent and in-depth discussion on "moral aspects of regime legitimacy" in Chapter 7, "Civil Military Operations and the War for Moral Legitimacy", in *Military Review*, (January 1988), pp. 36–49.

5. Paul G. Buchanan, "From Military Rule in Argentina and Brazil," *Authoritarian Regimes in Transition*, ed. Hans Binnendijk (Foreign Service Institute, Department of State: June 1987), p. 224.

6. Peter G. Snow, "Argentina: Development and Decay," *Latin America: Its Problems and Its Promises*, ed. Jan Knippers Black, (Boulder: Westview Press, 1984), p. 445.

7. P. H. Vigor, *A Guide to Marxism*, (New York: Humanities Press Inc., 1966), p. 87.

8. David B. Ottaway, "Constraints on U.S Involvement in Third World Protracted Warfare," Presentation, Sixteenth Annual Conference, International Security Studies Program, The Fletcher School of Law and Diplomacy, 1986.

9. Max G. Manwaring, *A Model For The Analysis of Insurgencies*, Report developed for the Small Wars Operations Research Directorate, US Southern Command, February 1987. (See Chapter 2 for his discussion of legitimacy in the context of contemporary warfare).

10. Howard J. Wriada, "Misreading Latin America—Again," *Foreign Policy*, 5, (Winter 1986–1987), p. 149.

11. Glen C. Dealy, "The Pluralistic Latins," *Foreign Policy*, 57, (Winter 1984–1985), pp. 116–117.

12. Ibid.

13. Ibid, p. 114.

14. M.A. Selisson and John A. Booth, eds., *Participation in Latin America*, Volume II (New York: Holmes and Myer, 1979), p. 200.

15. Dealy, "Pluralistic Latins," p. 110.

16. Oral interview with Alvaro Magana, conducted by Dr. Max G. Manwaring and translated by A.E. Letzer for the Small Wars Operations Research Directorate, U.S. Southern Command, El Salvador, February 1987.

17. Oral interview with Jose Napoleon Duarte, conducted by Dr. Max G. Manwaring and translated by A.E. Letzer for the Small Wars Operations Research Directorate U.S. Southern Command, El Salvador, November 1987.

18. Jean-Jacques Rousseau, "The Social Contract," *Great Books of the Western World*, Volume 38, (Chicago: Encyclopedia Britannica, 1952), p. 4.

19. Dealy, "Pluralistic Latins", p. 111.

20. Ralph Lee Woodward, "The Rise (and Fall) of Liberalism in El Salvador

and Nicaragua," *Authoritarian Regimes in Transition*, ed. by Hans Binnendijk, Foreign Service Institute, Department of State: June 1987), p. 116.

21. Ibid.

22. Paul G. Buchanan in his article, "From Military Rule in Argentina and Brazil," proposes a very useful distinction between liberalization and democratization. Liberalization refers to a process of relaxation and an opening up of decision-making spheres. It involves a broadening dialogue between the outgoing authoritarian regime and various political actors over the future course of society. This dialogue is marked by a piecemeal granting of procedural concessions. It is largely an internal dynamic. Democratization refers to the expansion of political participation through competitive elections and the rebirth of civil society—most evident in the reestablishment of collective identities and in the voicing of interests and demands on the part of social groups represented by organized agents. Democratization is very much an external dynamic that is often a response to liberalization.

23. Russell H. Fitzgibbon, *Latin America: A Panorama of Contemporary Politics*, (New York: Meredith Corporation, 1971), p. 27.

24. In Peru, there has been some success with the application of the New England model. From independence until 1919, between 1963 and 1968, and from 1980 to present, the model more or less applies. The dual system of government planning and administration has had varying results and is questionably efficient, however, the system does exist and supports the democratic idea of pluralism. For more in-depth information on Peru, see John T. Fishel, *Politics and Progress in the Peruvian Sierra*, Ph.D. Dissertation, Bloomington, Indiana, 1971, and in M. A. Selisso and John A. Booth, eds., *Participation in Latin America*, Vol I, (New York: Holmes and Myer, 1979).

25. Dealy, "Pluralistic Latins", p. 114.

26. Fitzgibbon, *Latin America: A Panorama*, p. 487.

27. Jose Napoleøn Duarte, "The People Will Decide Which Revolution,"*El Salvador at War: An Oral History*, ed. by Max G. Manwaring and Court Prisk (Washington D.C: National Defense University Press, 1988), p. 16.

28. Jan Knippers Black, "Participation and Political Process," *Latin America: Its Problems and Its Promises*, ed. by Jan Knippers Black, (Boulder: Westview Press, 1984), p. 168. Note: Increasing participation through interest groups and political parties is becoming a factor in influencing the national government. In the sense that these interest groups represent a geographical identity or political agenda they are considered in the context of a societal institution. Chambers of Commerce, Lions, or Kiwanis clubs in many Latin American countries fall in this category.

29. Dealy, "Pluralistic Latins," p. 116.

30. Charles de Secondat Baron de Montesquieu, "The Spirit of Laws," *Great Books of the Western World*, Volume 37, (Chicago: Encyclopedia Britannica, 1952), p. 146.

31. Robert Kennedy and Gabriel Marcella, "U.S. Security Interests on the Southern Flank: Interest—Challenges—Responses," in James R. Greene and

Brent Scowcroft, eds., *Report of the Atlantic Council's Working Group on the Caribbean Basin*, (Boston: Oelgeschlager, Gunn and Hain, 1984).

32. Irving S. Shapiro, "The Process," *Harvard Business Review*, November/December, 1979, p. 383.

33. Theodore Friend, "Marcos and the Philippines," *Orbis*, 32, No.4, (Fall 1988), p. 575.

34. John T. Fishel and Courtney E. Prisk, "A Strategy for Legitimacy," *Sword Papers*, Vol III, developed for the Small Wars Operations Research Directorate, U.S. Southern Command, February 1987.

35. Shapiro, "The Process," p. 386.

36. Jeffery W. Barrett, "Avoiding More Nicaraguas," *The Washington Quarterly*, II, No.4, (Autumn 1988), p. 174.

37. Fred Strum, "Philosophy and the Intellectual Tradition," *Latin America: Its Problems and Its Promises*, ed. Jan Knippers Black, (Boulder: Westview Press, 1984), p. 91.

38. Tommie Sue Montgomery, "El Salvador: The Roots of the Revolution," *Central America: Crisis and Adaptation*, ed. Steve C. Ropp and James A. Morris, (Albuquerque: University of New Mexico Press, 1984), p. 77.

39. Friend, "Marcos and the Philippines," p. 583.

40. Julio Castellano-Cambranes, "Origins of the Crisis of the Established Order in Guatemala," trans. David O. Wise, in *Central America Crisis and Adaptation*, ed. Steve C. Ropp and James A. Morris, (Albuquerque: University of New Mexico Press, 1984), p. 149, and Riordan Roett, "Peru: The Message From Garcia," *Foreign Affairs*, 64, No.2, (Winter 1985–1986), p. 277.

41. Buchanan, "From Military Rule," p. 225.

42. Jorge Nef, "Political Trends in Latin America: A Structure and Historical Analysis," *Latin America: Its Problems and Its Promise*, ed. Jan Knippers Black, (Boulder: Westview Press, 1984), p. 198.

43. Buchanan, "From Military Rule," p. 225.

44. Richard C. Brown, "Liberation Theology in Latin America: Its Challenges to the United States", *Conflict,* 4, No.1, 1983, p. 25.

45. Ibid, p. 53.

46. Frank K. Flinn, "Liberation Theology and Political Order in Latin America," *Spirit Matters: The Worldwide Impact of Religion on Contemporary Politics*, ed. Richard L. Rubenstein, (New York: Paragon House Publisher, 1987), p. 327.

47. Brown, "Liberation Theology in Latin America," p. 35.

48. Flinn, "Liberation Theology and Political Order," p. 322. Note Flinn and several other authors use "preservationist" stance or posture to mean those actions taken to maintain existing Church power and to ensure institutional survivability.

49. Eric A. Nordlinger, *Soldiers in Politics: Military Coups and Governments.* (Englewood Cliffs: Prentice-Hall, 1977), p. 3.

50. Lyle M. McAlister, et al., *The Military in Latin American Sociopolitical Evolution: Four Case Studies.* (Washington, D.C: Center for Research in Social Systems, 1970), p. 117

51. Nordlinger, *Soldiers in Politics*, p. 56.

52. Dealy, "Pluralistic Latins," p. 117.

53. Nordlinger, *Soldiers in Politics*, p. 557.

54. Robert Gilmore, *Caudillism and Militarism in Venezuela*, (Athens: Ohio University Press, 1964), p. 18.

55. John H. Herz, *From Dictatorship to Democracy: Coping with the Legacies of Authoritarianism and Totalitarianism*. (Westport: Greenwood Press, 1982), p. 281.

56. Myron Weiner, "Empirical Democratic Theory and Transition From Authoritarianism to Democracy," *PS*, XX, No.4, (Fall 1987), p. 863.

57. Fishel and Cowan, "Civil Military Operations," p.6.

58. Nordlinger, *Soldiers in Politics*, p. 76; Montgomery, "El Salvador: The Roots," p. 84; and Cesar Quintero, head of the Electoral College in Panama for 1984, interviewed in October 1988.

59. Henry Kissinger, *American Foreign Policy*, (New York: Norton, 1977), pp. 124–125.

60. Manwaring, *A Model*, p. 18.

61. Friend, "Marcos and the Philippines," and Barrett, "Avoiding More Nicaraguas," p. 18.

62. Castellano-Cambranes, "Origins of the Crisis," p. 146.

63. Stephen M. Gorman, "Nicaragua" in *Central America: Crisis and Adaption*, ed. Steve C. Ropp and James A. Morris. (Albuquerque: University of New Mexico Press, 1984), p. 53.

64. Ibid.

65. Thomas Hobbs, "The Leviathan," *Great Books of the Western World*, Volume 23 (Chicago: Encyclopedia Britannica, 1952), p. 157.

66. The history of the judiciary in Latin America varies greatly from region to region. In Argentina and Chile, the judiciary enjoys the reputation of being relatively independent and effective. In Brazil, Colombia, and Ecuador, there have been periods of executive control and questionable independence, but for the most part the judiciary is considered independent and effective. In Central America, the judiciary has been controlled by the executive and has questionable power to act independently from or in opposition to the executive.

67. Friend, "Marcos and the Philippines," p. 579; "Humans Rights in Panama," Americas Watch Committee, 1988; and Fitzgibbon, *Latin America: Panorama*, p. 320.

68. Barrett, "Avoiding More Nicaraguas," p. 21.

69. Eliot A. Cohen, "Constraints on America's Conduct of Small Wars," *International Security*, 9, No. 2, (Fall 1984), p. 169.

70. Clifford Krauss, "Revolution in Central America," *Foreign Affairs: America and the World*, (1986), p. 5572.

71. Duarte, "The People Will Decide Which Revolution," p. 16.

72. Ottaway, "Constraints on U.S. Involvement," p. 18

7

Other Actions That Make a Difference: The Case of Peru

Max G. Manwaring, Courtney E. Prisk, and John T. Fishel

Modern multidimensional insurgencies operate on two levels. The first is generally long-term and strategic. Although also strategically important, the second level deals with more immediate and more operational efforts. As each dimension is highly interrelated, there is also a strong correlation between both levels of activity in this type of conflict.[1]

The first level of concern has to do with the primary political-strategic efforts necessary to achieve ultimate success against a determined domestic foe. They include the necessary organization to ensure unity of effort, the operationalization of the concept of WILL, and the umbrella of legitimacy. The second level includes factors that can also be very political and strategic in an insurgency, but are more often categorized as military and operational.

In any case, both aspects are extremely important in the win or lose outcome of any internal conflict. That is to say, one can concentrate on the longer-term aspects of the conflict and be destroyed by the quicker, more militant actions of and adversary before the more strategic factors can be completely and effectively operationalized. Or, on the other hand, one can do everything well in the short term (e.g., win all the battles) but if the long term is ignored or given too low a priority the war can be lost. What is required is a balance of the various first and second level counter-insurgency activities across the board.

The three "second level" factors and their component parts postulated below relate to "the guerrilla war", "the war against subversion", and "the war to limit support for the insurgency". In examining the situation in contemporary Peru, we find that these wars within a general insurgency war have played major roles in the ongoing struggle. Adherence to these fundamentals suggested here would help ensure that counterinsurgency efforts center around the appropriate operational means by which a subversive element and its support mechanisms might be neutralized. Lack of adherence to these dimensions of conflict only shortens the time before the moment of truth. As *Sendero Luminoso's* Abimael Guzman (President Gonzalo) has said, "Except for Power, everything else is illusion."[2]

The Guerrilla War

Military success in this type of warfare is dependent upon highly mobile, well trained, disciplined, properly equipped, and motivated troops working political and psychological as well as associated military goals. The traditional norms and existing mobile assets of an insurgent-targeted country's armed forces usually fall short of these requirements. If they were adequate, the insurgency would probably be under control and virtually nonthreatening. A foreign power can help change the situation, but ultimately—in a nationalistic milieu such as that of Peru—the targeted country must strengthen its own civil and military capability.[3]

This capability can be defined by three conditional measures:

Understanding the Phenomenon. The study of the fundamental nature of conflict has always been recognized as an important step toward the understanding of conventional war, and it is no less relevant to insurgency. This is a factor that concerns all senior civilian and military decision makers. It involves gaining knowledge of the nature of insurgency—with particular reference to the way in which force can be employed to achieve political ends, and the way in which political considerations affect the use of force. General John R. Galvin summarized the concept in the following terse statement: "In this kind of war you need to be able to do more than pull a trigger."[4]

It appears that the principal Peruvian advisors, leaders, and commanders understand the problem in the rhetorical sense. However, that rhetorical understanding has not been translated into an operational program to counter the multidimensional nature of "revolutionary war." Within this context, the Garcia regime—as well as its predecessors—has tended to ignore the political, economic, social, and moral aspects of the threat and has chosen to consider it a strictly military problem. Even with an increased awareness of the phenomenon and a presidential call to combat it more effectively,[5] the operationalization and implementation components of the counterinsurgency process have not been adequately pursued at the strategic and operational levels.[6]

From the strictly military perspective, the Peruvian High Command appears to have some of the same problems. It, too, has tended to ignore the insurgency. In spite of eight years of trying to pacify ever-expanding Emergency Zones, the major part of the military establishment remains oriented toward the conventional low probability threat represented by Chile and Ecuador.

When the High Command does respond to the internal problem, it appears do so while ignoring its own counter insurgency "campaign plan". Moreover, it would appear that the officers and the units involved against the insurgency do not understand at least two basic things:

First they demonstrate little understanding of the way in which force can be employed to achieve political and psychological ends, and the way in which political considerations affect the use of force.

Second, they demonstrate little ability to execute the combination of civil and military measures required to achieve the strategic or operational objectives of the "campaign plan."[7] If these elements were understood, the atrocities that have taken place would not have occurred, the insurgents would have lost much of their popular support, and general security would be adequate to allow the implementation of political, economic, and social measures against the basic causes of the insurgency.

Finally, there are tactical military aspects of the counterinsurgency (e.g., ambushes, constant interdiction of enemy routes, and patrolling) that could produce a decided advantage over the insurgent military forces. However, even if the Peruvian military forces were adequately instructed in these activities, they generally do not have the opportunity to utilize this knowledge.[8] In order to "close with and destroy the enemy", one must know who the enemy is and where he is. This has not been the case in Peru in the past, and it does not appear to be the case now. Thus, whole villages become targets in the wanton hope that "maybe five or six of the hundred or so dead will be insurgents". What of the others? "They are only Indians; who cares?"[9]

If there is one fundamental reason why the insurgents are winning in Peru and why the government and its armed forces are losing the "low intensity conflict" there, it is that the civil-military leadership does not understand what it is they are up against.

Training and Motivation. Counterinsurgency training must be far more than technically proficient. It must also establish an understanding of the nonmilitary aspects of violence, an appreciation of human rights, a belief in the correctness of the cause, a confidence in ultimate victory, and a willingness to accept hardship in pursuit of clearly defined and just ends. These are not easy tasks, but they are necessary if the armed forces "are to become part of the solution, not part of the problem".[10]

The Peruvian armed forces have been trained for the conventional war against the traditional Chilean and/or Ecuadoran threats. In these terms, it is well understood that Peruvian forces are dedicated to a legitimate cause and against a well-defined and easily identified enemy. In this, they have been aided by significant amounts of Soviet training, equipment, and technical assistance.[11] There is no evidence that the Soviets have taught the Peruvians anything about insurgency or counterinsurgency or equipped them for that type of effort. Whether this is a sin of omission or commission is moot.

The essential point is that the Peruvian armed forces—in general terms—are not trained, not motivated, and not properly equipped or organized for an insurgent war. The same deficiencies apply to any kind of war in the Peruvian highlands—which would be considerably different than the tank warfare on the coastal plain and deserts for which they are prepared. In addition, it appears that the Peruvian forces are unable to define the internal enemy.[12] Clearly, they have a long way to go toward achieving educational, training, and equipment needs for an effective guerrilla war.

Mobility. Insurgent military centers of gravity are normally not easily accessible. The military force given the mission to destroy them must have the assets necessary to get to the enemy virtually anywhere. In Peru, that means the ability to operate and communicate in every possible climate, in extremely remote areas, and at altitudes up to 14,000 and 15,000 feet above sea level. Even the best informed, best trained, and most highly motivated military force cannot be effective if unable to get to its targets. Thus, a successful counter-insurgency strategy must include mobility assets.

As noted above, the Peruvian armed forces are generally equipped to fight a conventional war in the deserts and coastal areas along the Pacific Ocean. Yet, the inability to bring forces against guerrilla units or to exploit insurgent vulnerabilities rapidly cannot be overcome by simply reallocating resources from the Chilean and Ecuadoran frontiers. That equipment is as inappropriate to insurgency war in the highlands as conventional training and organization of the troops is for that situation.[13] The lack of mobility assets is perhaps the greatest weakness in the Peruvian capability to defeat the insurgents militarily.

In sum, neither the civilian nor the military leadership in Peru has shown that it understands the essential dualities of the country that have driven and compounded the insurgency. These dualities include the contrasts between the Indian and Mestizo cultures, the coast and the highlands, and rhetoric and action. There appears little appreciation that an insurgency is fought on diverse fronts, or that troops must do more than kill Indians in order to win the long-term struggle over who governs the country. As a result, the armed forces have not even begun the first assault on the insurgent military centers of gravity.

The War Against Subversion

The principal components of this dimension of insurgency, then, are:

Neutralizing the Insurgent Leadership. This is the one way that the fundamental insurgency can be quickly altered to the advantage of a targeted government. Thus, a primary objective in a counterinsurgency effort has got to be the neutralization or elimination of the guerrilla leadership and organizational structure. Successfully attacking the leadership—physically, and psychologically—results in elimination of centralized direction, fragmentation of the control mechanisms, and ultimate destruction of the entire organization.

Despite a few successes and at least one notable arrest of the supposed Number Two in the Sendero Luminoso organization, the insurgent leadership and structure remain relatively unchallenged. As an example, no one seems to know if "President Gonzalo" is alive or dead; no one seems to know if he is in Peru or not; and, no one can even provide a picture of him that is less than twenty years old.[14] Obviously, leadership can be replaced.

However, if those individuals who represent continuity and longevity of effort were to be neutralized, the organization could not be as effective as before. This component of the countersubversion cannot be classified as anything but a failure in Peru. If the incumbent government is going to stop the tide of insurgency, the "vanguard of the proletariat" must be targeted as a primary center of gravity.

Recognizing the Importance of Intelligence. It must be the aim of the government to develop the fullest details of the entire revolutionary movement with a consistent view toward neutralizing it.[15] This capability involves active support of intelligence operations as a dominant element of both strategy and tactics. It requires the establishment of strategic, operational, and tactical user-level capabilities that include the collection, fusion, and analysis of ALL sources of information. It requires a network focused on production and rapid dissemination of timely intelligence. Furthermore, it demands an effective interrogation capability at the operational and tactical levels to take full advantage of human intelligence sources.[16]

The capabilities outlined above are not expensive in dollar terms but, in the Peruvian context they require rethinking of the use of violence in intelligence collection; fusing of the various types of intelligence; horizontal and vertical disseminating in a timely manner to include increasing intelligence communication resources for "user" units; and developing effective operations security and counterintelligence measures. [17]

Moreover, all these measures will remain ineffective and no useful human source intelligence will be forthcoming until the military can guarantee adequate protection, civil-military operations, and treatment for the Indians as real human beings. Until these things are done, commanders will continue to fight "in the dark" against an enemy who is "ten feet tall". That is to say, they will be unable to determine who the enemy is; they will not know where the enemy is; they will be ignorant of enemy strengths and weaknesses; and they will remain unable to find out.

Developing the Necessary Psychological/Public Diplomacy and Civil Affairs Organization and Effort. A major by-product of developing the fullest details of the insurgent organizational infrastructure can be an understanding of strengths and vulnerabilities. This information can be exploited to discredit, neutralize, and eventually eliminate the various components of a subversive movement. This can be done on the battlefield, within a country, and internationally. However, it requires the establishment of international, national, regional, and local capabilities that include the utilization of all elements of the media and a first-rate public relations effort.

Again, in the Peruvian context, these actions require the rethinking and reallocation of priorities and resources. Evidence indicates that this component of the struggle is understood rhetorically, but that understanding has not been transformed into an action program.[18]

Another part of the war against subversion that could act as a major force multiplier is that of military civic action in support of a national development program. In this regard, two broad categories of civic action exist—mitigating and developmental. The former is a short-term humanitarian assistance effort designed to mitigate the negative effects of specific military actions. Developmental civic action is the type of program through which long-term positive objectives can be achieved.[19] Despite the fact that General Edgardo Mercado Jarrin pointed out the importance of this type of action over twenty years ago, in Peru,[20] neither mitigating nor developmental civic action appears to receive the kind of attention or priority that is required for any degree of success in the counterinsurgency environment.[21]

Operationally, the War Against Subversion dimension of insurgency war has not been adequately pursued in Peru. As a matter of fact, it is one of the more significant failures.

The War to Limit Support for the Insurgency

Internal and external support is as important to an insurgent organization as it is to a targeted government. Once an insurgent organization is firmly established within a society, it is not enough for a government to foster the military capability to destroy an enemy; it is not enough to work for reform and to reinforce governmental legitimacy; it is not enough to organize for the conflict; and, it is not enough to obtain large quantities of outside aid. The insurgents must be separated from their primary sources of physical and psychological strength—whoever and wherever they may be.

External Support. Sendero Luminoso claims that it receives no assistance from any outside source. It is argued that over the past twenty-five or so years, Sendero has developed a basis of support in the Peruvian highlands making external support unnecessary.[22] Indeed, nationalistic "Indianist" rhetoric would make such support illegitimate and unwelcome.[23] On the other hand, the "revisionist" Tupac Amaro (MRTA) organization reportedly receives help from such diverse sources as Cuba, Nicaragua, Colombia's M-19 insurgent organization, Ecuador's "Alfaro Vive Carajo" group, and various narco-traffickers.[24]

The Need to Eliminate Sanctuaries. Any given insurgent organization can exist as long as it has access to rest, medical attention, training, and resupply. This requirement for safe havens was the basis for Sendero Luminoso's spending nearly twenty years in the preparatory "strategic equilibrium" and in the establishment of a primary support mechanism in the Party organization and of the integral support organization within the military part of the Sendero structure. It is also the basis of the strategy of establishing and consolidating bases of support as the final stage in the program for besieging the cities and bringing about the total collapse of the State.[25] There is no evidence that this aspect of the counterinsurgency has been addressed in the Peruvian case. Portions of the country are perceived to have been ceded to the insurgents either because those areas are too difficult to control or because they are considered to be unimportant. In either case, the government has lost credibility and Sendero Luminoso is almost completely free to move about the country.

Either through intimidation or cooperation they have been able to extract money, food, and other resources from the general population with relative ease. Aside from relatively rigorous attempts to control key traffic points throughout the country, the issue of isolating insurgents from their bases of support has not been addressed in the Peruvian conflict.[26]

Conclusion

The general war in Peru is being won by the insurgents. Government attempts to win the guerrilla war, the war against subversion, and the war to limit insurgent support have fallen short. As a result, it is questionable as to whether Peru—without positive, serious, and quick action directed at resolving these problems—can regain the initiative.

Notes

1. Max G. Manwaring, "A Statistical Model for the Analysis of Internal Conflicts", unpublished manuscript, dated 31 Jan 90.
2. "El Documento Oficial de Sendero," in Rogger Mercado U., *Los Partidos Politicos en el Peru*, (Lima: Ediciones Latinamericanos, 1985), p. 110.
3. Col Robert M. Herrick and Col Max G. Manwaring, "A Threat Oriented Strategy for Conflict Control," *Military Review*, (July 1987): pp. 14–16.
4. Interview with General John R. Galvin by Max G. Manwaring on 18 August 1987 in Mons, Belgium. Also see "An Exclusive AFJ Interview with General John R. Galvin, USA, Commander-in-Chief, US Southern Command," *Armed Forces Journal*, (December 1985): pp. 35–42.
5. Reported in *Expreso*, 15 de abril 1988, p. E-4.
6. The assertions made here and below regarding the Peruvian conduct of the counterinsurgency are the result of interviews with approximately 50 lieutenant colonels and colonels, and their naval equivalents, conducted over the period 16–20 May 1988, in Lima, Peru by Max G. Manwaring. These assertions were corroborated in further discussions with other civilian and military leaders during 6–10 November 1989. These individuals have asked that a "non-attribution policy" be applied to them.
7. Ibid.
8. Ibid.
9. Ibid.
10. Interview with Colonel John D. Waghelstein, USA, commander of the 7th Special Forces Group, US Army, by Max G. Manwaring on 23 February 1987 in Washington, DC. Also see "Post-Vietnam Counterinsurgency Doctrine," *Military Review*, (May 1985): 40–49.
11. Manwaring interviews in Peru May 1988, and November 1989.
12. Ibid.
13. Ibid.

14. Ibid.

15. Sir Robert Thompson, *Revolutionary War in World Strategy, 1945–1969,* (New York: Taplinger Publishing Co., 1970), p. 8.

16. Herrick and Manwaring, "A Threat-Oriented Strategy": pp. 9–14.

17. Manwaring interviews in Peru May 1988, and November 1989.

18. Ibid.

19. This concept is developed in LTC John T. Fishel and Major Edmund S. Cowan, "Civil-Military Operations and the War for Legitimacy in Latin America," *Military Review* (January 1988): pp. 36–49.

20. General Edgardo Mercado Jarrin, "Insurgency in Latin America: Its Impact on Political and Military Strategy," *Military Review,* (March 1969), pp. 17–20. Note: this article was originally published in Peru in 1967.

21. Manwaring interviews in Peru 16–20 May 1988, and November 1989.

22. Ibid.; *Bases de Discussion* (Lima: Comite Central del Partido Comunista del Peru, September 1987), pp. 32–43; and *Desarrollar la Querra popular sirviendo a la Revolucion mundial,* (Lima: Comite Central del Partido Comunista del Peru, 1986), pp. 82–88.

23. Interestingly, Sendero Luminoso has not commented on the tacit/indirect support provided by the USSR as a result of NOT providing counterinsurgency assistance to the Peruvian government and armed forces. Also, there has been a significant increase in reports of Sendero arrangements with narco-traffickers. Although the nature and degree of such alleged cooperation are unclear, it must be considered as both an increase in Sendero resources and a potential vulnerability.

24. Raul Gonzalez, "Sendero: Los problemas de campo y de la ciudad . . . y ademas el MRTA," *Quehacer,* (enero–febrero 1988), pp. 47–62. Also see *Caretas,* 23 noviembre 1987, pp. 11–17; and, *Caretas,* 16 noviembre 1987, pp. 8C-17; 70.

25. "El Discurso del Dr. Guzman," in Mercado U., *Los Partidos Politicos,* pp. 85–90.

26. Manwaring interviews in Peru, May 1988, and November 1989.

PART THREE

Conclusions and Implications

8

The Need for Strategic Perspective: Insights from El Salvador

Max G. Manwaring and Courtney E. Prisk

To provide a better understanding of the most likely type of challenge to United States' leadership over the near to long term, we examine the situation in El Salvador in terms of strategic "lessons learned." This is done in order to avoid specific and often random facts that might be made into some sort of template—memorized and applied too easily—without proper reflection or sufficiently rigorous analysis of the situation. We do this not so much as to relive history unlearned as to focus on the broad, significant themes and questions which promote that invaluable mental power we call judgment.

With this in mind, we have endeavored to explore the phenomenon of the conflict and some of the major contours of the war as they have developed in El Salvador since 1979. We are not attempting to give a short history of the struggle in that country, but only an elaboration of what certain key individuals think about the war—what they think are the really important lessons. That is, what they think they have learned, what they think the country's leadership has learned, what they think the various entities involved in the war have learned about the strategic nature of the struggle.

An Overview of the War in El Salvador

In the late 1970s, chronic political, economic, and social problems created by a self-serving, military-supported oligarchy began to generate another in a long list of crises in El Salvador. During that time, General Carlos Humberto Romero was brought to power by those who thought that he would be able to establish a regime strong enough to protect the interests of the oligarchy and to control the various forces agitating for change. Yet by 1979, the situation was beyond control by repression.

The catalyst that ignited the continuing violence in El Salvador was the military coup of October 1979 in which Romero was ousted as the last protector of the interests of the oligarchy. After that, the history of the country breaks down into four clearly defined periods. The period after the coup was one of almost complete disarray. None of the three major actors in the conflict—the military, the insurgents, and the United States—was ready for the aftermath of fifty years of authoritarian government. Then, from the end of 1981 to the end of 1984, the Salvadoran revolutionaries seemed to unify and appeared to be well on their way to a military victory and the assumption of political power in their own right. Clearly, the insurgents were ascendant. By the end of 1984, however, the armed forces had taken the best the insurgents could give and were beginning to regain control of the political-military situation. Perhaps it is still too early to tell, but the period 1985–1987 appears to be the beginning of the end of the idea that revolution comes only from the "barrel of a gun." The war had changed direction. Finally, the period from 1987 to the present has been a time in which nothing really decisive seems to have taken place. There have been some spectacular events, but the revolutionaries have been deprived of their military victory. The United States–backed Salvadoran forces have not won either. There is an impasse within a protracted war.

Before examining the military-historical divisions of the Salvadoran conflict and the major insights derived from each, let us consider the context of that struggle. It provides an elaboration of the central strategic problem that permeates the entire war.

The Context of the War

The guerrilla war in El Salvador began in the early 1960's in response to the abusive and repressive nature of the successive governments which had been essentially at the service of the Salvadoran oligarchy. Through the Salvadoran Communist Party (PCES) efforts, the National University became a center for agitation and change. The PCES, once having subverted the university, began to successfully promote the Marxist-Leninist ideas of preparing the people, subverting the political parties, disrupting the functioning of government, and agitating through demonstrations. This militant but relatively non-violent strategy seemed to have worked when the coalition of the PCES, the National Revolutionary Movement (MNR) and Christian Democratic Party (PDC) won the 1972 presidential election. But, when the election was taken away by fraud the PCES strategy fell apart and a new set of more combative radicals began to espouse violent armed confrontation. As the resultant demonstrations, riots, strikes, and chaos grew in intensity, the government became more repressive.[1] El Salvador was almost literally in flames.

By 1979, it was clear to even the most obtuse that the country was either going to follow the way of Nicaragua or Chile. The military-civil junta which generated the 1979 coup chose to attempt a modification of the Chilean model. Like the insurgents, the junta saw the need for radical change. However, instead of attempting to achieve that change through revolutionary violence, it proposed a set of dynamic, evolutionary processes to correct the existing problems and leave the general fabric of society intact. These changes would be accomplished through a "democratic process" in which the long-repressed people could take a major role.[2]

Speaking for the insurgents, Dr. Guillermo M. Ungo saw the legitimacy of the regime as the primary strategic problem in El Salvador.[3] The former provisional president of El Salvador, Dr. Alvaro Magana agreed. He argues that the junta, which included Jose Napoleon Duarte, understood the strategic nature of the problem and countered with a program designed to nullify the efforts of the extreme left. "The development of a relatively honest and competent government interested in the welfare of the people—what you call legitimacy—was indeed crucial to Salvadoran stability and security."[4]

The third actor in the struggle, the United States, tended to view the situation in El Salvador solely as an extension of the general East-West superpower confrontation, and as a follow-on to the Sandinista takeover in Nicaragua. As such, the primary objective of the United States seemed to be to do what was necessary to return to "normalcy" so as to concentrate on the primary threat.[5]

The context of the war in El Salvador, then, was twofold. In terms of time, it would be a long-term struggle for survival for both the revolutionaries and for the government. As far as the United States was concerned, it was something to be resolved as quickly as possible, but with complacence. In terms of perspective, the conflict for both insurgent and incumbent would be a total political and moral, as well as military, effort. Only an outside superpower would have the luxury of thinking in "limited" terms.

In sum, the thrust of the revolutionary program centered around the redress of real as well as perceived grievances and deprivations. The government counterinsurgency planners understood this and did not respond only to the "enemy" military force and the guerrilla war.

They centered their efforts around basic reforms and the establishment of the foundations of participatory democracy.[6] Thus, the Legitimacy War (the achievement and maintenance of the moral right to govern) was considered to be the major concern upon which everything depended, and the basic context of the conflict.[7]

Disarray: A Look at the Antagonists During 1979–1981

In late 1979, the guerrillas initiated a series of indirect and direct attacks throughout the country. The first type of attack was an intensive psychological campaign to challenge the legitimacy of the Romero regime and the *junta* that succeeded him. Then, in January 1981, the insurgents attempted a "final offensive" in the hope of gaining a quick and total military victory. The effort was unsuccessful and was rationalized as the beginning of a "general offensive" which would ultimately lead to the final objective—to bring down the government.[8]

Some of the Salvadoran military saw the forces of change moving out of control at about the same time. Moreover, they saw and understood what had happened to General Somoza's National Guard at the hands of the Nicaraguan people. The parallels were hard to ignore, and the general conclusion was that the Salvadoran armed forces would suffer similar consequences if they did not act quickly to put out the fire of revolution in their own country.[9] To save their institution (and themselves) they would have to break the alliance with the oligarchy and realign with political forces that could win popular support.[10]

These officers were buffeted by both the left and the right, and also internally. The right opposed them because the officers were tied to the oligarchic interests that were threatened by proposed reforms.[11] They were labeled as traitors by the left because they were co-opting the political-social rationale of the Marxist-Leninist movement.[12] That rationale was placed within a context in which the civil-military elites could not possibly make "correct" interpretations of and solutions to the country's problems because they must be the "vanguard of the proletariat" who would make those interpretations and determine proper solutions. Internally, within the armed forces themselves, the need to implement fundamental reforms, coupled with the struggle to establish a government based on a nontraditional, noncorporate model, created confusion and fragmentation.[13]

These problems and their components were magnified by the inability of the civil-military junta to cope with the war of information. This inability had an impact on the general war in two ways. First, it gave the insurgents—traditionally better prepared to fight a propaganda war—a veneer of cohesion, strength, and even legitimacy.[14] Perhaps more importantly, it caused United States policy-makers—ever sensitive to the media image of an ally—to waver on the type and amount of support to provide. Jose Napoleon Duarte recognized the strategic implications of the issue: "Overall, we were being crushed under the avalanche of international press coverage. We had been totally unprepared for it. If there had been some structure to handle the press, some capacity to investigate charges and demonstrate what was true or false, we might have done better."[15] As it was, "FMLN propaganda almost defeated us by itself."[16]

In the time-honored tradition of Latin American politics, the dominant military leadership sought to establish a civil-military junta. This effort focused on sharing power with as many of the key power centers in the country as were willing to cooperate in an attempt to establish a unified control of the situation against the militant left. This would provide the basis for the subsequent organization that would have to be established and empowered to pursue the political-military dimensions of the struggle effectively. Putting the concept of unity of command into effect would help ensure that all civil-military activity would be concentrated on the ultimate goal—survival.[17] The difficulty of achieving this goal when faced with an enemy specifically attempting to fragment and subvert a society can indeed be considered an organizational war.[18]

The United States, for the Salvadoran reformers, was the only source of external support that could make a difference. Yet, during this period of disarray, the U.S. was also apparently confused.[19] This problem is highlighted by the unwillingness or inability of senior policy-makers to develop any kind of coordinated effort to deal with the situation in El Salvador—despite the general willingness and commitment of both the Carter and the Reagan administrations to help.[20]

The perceived "too little, too late" conundrum during this crucial period is but one example. The argument made by Dr. Alvaro Magana, who acted as President during 1982–1984, is that there appears to have been no agreed, coherent strategy to achieve objectives; indeed, no agreement as to those objectives. Decisions concerning the allocation of "North American" resources to El Salvador appear to have been made on the basis of what the minimum effort was that could be made while maintaining congressional support for administration policy. As a matter of fact, the only alternative policies examined involved different force levels for the Salvadoran army and specific amounts of economic and military aid.[21] Thus, issues addressed and decisions made were always tactical and short-term in nature—the typical bureaucratic "in-box drill" of finding a "quick-fix," selling it, and getting rid of the immediate problem.

Finally, despite 15 or more years of preparatory work and the decision to try to take control of the country, the revolutionary movement was not ready to take advantage of the near anarchy of the time. The various revolutionary factions that made up the FMLN (Faribundo Marti Liberation Movement) had not yet unified in any significant way. Thus, to both insurgents and incumbents, the strategic solution to the mutual problems of confusion and disarray was to begin to create a real unity of command and effort.[22] Both parties recognized that without a body at the highest level that can establish, enforce, and continually refine cogent objectives, authority is fragmented and there is no way to resolve the myriad problems endemic to war and survival. That could mean failure, or at best, no win for either side. Again, only the United States had the luxury of ignoring the central reality of the period—the need for an organizational structure with the authority to plan and implement the entire counterinsurgency assistance effort.

The Period of Insurgent Ascendancy: 1981–1984

The leadership of the Popular Liberation Forces (FPL), the largest of the guerrilla groups within the FMLN, understood the importance of moral power in the strategy of conflict. They were also responsive to the need to operationalize the classical principle of unity of command in war; e.g., engage in the organizational war. Nevertheless, the more military-oriented leadership of the People's Revolutionary Army (ERP), flush with the insurrectionist victory of The Sandinistas and supported by a strong push from the Cubans, prevailed. They elected to do two things. First, they decided to maintain five separate armed elements and give the FMLN organization only umbrella status.[23] Then they determined to pursue a quick military victory over what was perceived to be a completely incompetent enemy.

Despite the failure of what was called the "final offensive" of January 1981, the FMLN had sufficient organizational unity, manpower, arms, sanctuaries, and outside support to generate a more-or-less continuous and growing military effort from the end of 1981 to the end of 1984. During that period, they were able to organize, train, and logistically support units that were capable of mounting attacks with as many as 600 men at virtually any time. They were also capable of controlling large portions of the national territory during that period.[24]

Given the admittedly poor internal support given to the guerrillas on the part of the Salvadoran people, the ability to achieve this level of warfare is remarkable. This degree of military capability can only be explained in terms of the great amounts of external support enjoyed by the militant left.

Conversely, the external support enjoyed by the FMLN can also be explained by the failure to understand, support, or engage appropriate efforts by either the Salvadoran government or its North American ally in the war against external support. Rather than actively attempt to counter the flow of arms and material, the Salvadoran security organizations and their mentors from the United States concentrated their primary efforts on finding a "smoking gun" that would clearly and legally implicate Nicaragua, Cuba, North Vietnam, and/or the Soviet Union in the support of the Salvadoran guerrillas.[25]

Despite the employment of various sophisticated and costly "platforms" directed against possible means and routes of entry into Salvador, the effort never did establish the credibility of the "smoking gun" argument. Moreover, by ignoring or refusing to engage the guerrillas' sources of support, and the cross-border sanctuaries providing political and military life support to them, the United States and the Salvadoran government provided the insurgents with their own "protected Ho Chi Minh Trail." According to Joaquin Villalobos, this figurative trail was as important to the FMLN as the real trail was to the victory of the North in the Vietnamese struggle.[26] As a result, the flow of physical and psychological support to the FMLN from abroad was never seriously impaired.[27]

In support of this argument, Dr. Guillermo Ungo stated subtly that "FDR-FMLN efforts have received the deepest international support from a broad range of countries in both the capitalist and socialist worlds—from Cuba, France, Mexico, Nicaragua, Sweden, and Third World countries. . . . Even in the United States, important sectors of the population have a better understanding of the situation of the Salvadoran people and the reason for their political and armed struggle than does the United States Government."[28] Thus, when France and Mexico granted formal recognition to the guerrillas, it was easy to understand why Jose Napoleon Duarte considered it the low point in the conflict.[29]

The other parties to the conflict were not inactive, although the external support for a formidable guerrilla military effort was the most obvious and best-reported aspect of the period. In a struggle for the "hearts and minds" of a people, the fundamental question is one of rectitude. It was here that the government response began. While the "revolutionaries" were concentrating their efforts on the military aspects of the war, the Salvadoran leadership made the struggle to gain legitimacy—and, thus, internal and external support—their first priority.[30] As a consequence, one of the first things the civil-military junta did on taking control of the government after the 1979 coup was to announce land, banking, and commodity export reforms. Subsequently, other reforms were promulgated—not the least of which were popular elections that really mattered.[31] The degree of success these reforms and human rights enforcement may or may not enjoy today is moot. The point is that enough Salvadoran people have been sufficiently convinced of progress that they have not supported the insurgent cause to anywhere near the extent that might be expected.[32]

The armed forces' leadership responded to the legitimization process on at least two levels. First, they broke with their traditional right-wing allies and joined with moderate civilian politicians in an alliance to support the democratic process. The military went to extreme lengths to provide security for free elections, and has consistently demonstrated loyalty to civilian institutions—particularly to the office of the presidency. In the opinion of General Fred F. Woerner, this was probably the most significant reform of the decade.[33]

On the second level, the military leadership understood that this type of war must be fought on diverse fronts, and that soldiers and officers have got to do more than shoot people in order to win the long-term struggle.[34] Consequently, they took the necessary time and resources to begin to change an 11,000–14,000–man "Praetorian Guard" accustomed to abusing its authority into a more professional 50,000–55,000–man organization that could engage an enemy force without alienating the general citizenry. This was another significant reform with long-term, positive implications.[35] As far as the controlling military elite were concerned at that point, the central strategic effort could not be directed against a specific piece of territory or the enemy force—the primary center of gravity was the basic underpinnings of the Salvadoran government itself.[36]

Nevertheless, as the armed forces began the process of reform and professionalization, they also developed the ability to fight a relatively intense war.[37]

The role of the United States was a positive one in these terms. However, during the 1981–1984 period of insurgent ascendancy, United States' assistance left much to be desired. At least a few senior decision-makers were not particularly concerned. They assumed that once the United States government had showed that it was prepared to provide some help, the guerrilla movement would see the inevitability of defeat and simply go away.[38] What their assumption did not take into account was the ideological commitment of the FMLN hardcore membership, and the strategic importance of the Nicaraguan-Cuban-Vietnamese-Soviet connection. In short, there was no thorough analysis or appreciation of the situation.

However, it is necessary to point out that despite the fact that the Salvadoran government "never knew when the next shipment of ammunition would arrive," or what they could plan on in terms of other assistance, North American aid was as important to the government as the external support of its allies was to the insurgents.[39]

In summarizing this seemingly dark period in the history of the conflict in El Salvador, three things stand out in strategic perspective. First, legitimacy was reaffirmed as the factor that in the long-term would prove to be more decisive than traditional military action. The government and the armed forces got an apparently slow start in the military war against the insurgents but began the process of seizing the "moral high ground." On the other hand, the *comandantes* of the FMLN chose to all but ignore the counsel so generously provided by Mao, Giap, and their own "politicos" regarding the absolute need to supplement military action with a rigorous appreciation of the moral dimension of contemporary war.

Second, the classical principles of unity of command and objective are also reaffirmed in the obverse. Both sides organized only to the extent necessary for survival and perhaps even for moderate success, but not to the degree required to win. None of the principals was able to overcome their individual problems of turf, distrust, or lethargy to the degree necessary to develop an organization with the requisite authority to coordinate and implement a winning set of strategic military-political objectives. As an example of the North American situation, Ambassador Thomas Pickering states:

> We had neither the doctrine nor the support, nor the coordination in the United States government that would really be required to deal effectively with that kind of operation. I don't think we ever developed it; we still are kind of *ad hoc* in our way of viewing the problems. That is really quite a critical comment.[40]

Finally, although North American aid probably saved the incumbent Salvadoran government, outside aid made the guerrilla ascendancy possible. Yet, there appears to have been little cognizance of the war against external support. Neither the United States nor the Salvadoran government seriously addressed the external sources of insurgent support. What gave the FMLN the physical strength and psychological support in this context was not the assistance itself or the routes that assistance might have taken to get the battlefield. Rather, the center of gravity was and is the source of whatever support might be provided.[41]

The War Changes Direction

By the end of 1984, the FMLN had been forced to take the military defensive. As a result, the Salvadoran guerrillas prepared to initiate a psychological offensive against two primary targets. First, they refocused on the illegitimacy of the regime in power. Second, they began to mount a very strong attack against the government's source of power—the United States. The strategy became that of taking a low military profile, making an opening that would lead to negotiations, and working for U.S. disengagement from the conflict.[42]

In this connection, the attack on the Duarte government stressed the inability of the Christian Democratic regime to promulgate serious reforms in the system, to stem governmental and business corruption and fraud, and to bring to justice individuals known to have violated human rights. This campaign discredited the Duarte administration in the eyes of a large segment of the population, and began to disrupt the community of interest between the Salvadoran and United States governments.[43]

At the same time, the insurgents set out to attack the economic infrastructure, the transportation network, and local symbols of central government authority throughout the country. The primary objective of this "armed propaganda" was not military. Rather, it was to convince the population and the United States that the government continues to be incompetent or unwilling to provide an adequate security environment for the socio-economic development of El Salvador. Moreover, tying down regular military forces in the attempt to protect specific infrastructure and population centers allows the insurgents great latitude for political and psychological efforts in the rest of the country.[44]

Third, multiple calls for "cease fire" and various attempts to open a dialogue with the government have resulted in internal and external perceptions that the FMLN wants peace. In a country and a world tired of almost continual strife over the past several years, the appeal of peace at any cost is strong.[45]

Further, insurgent efforts to stem United States' assistance to El Salvador were and continue to be centered on the proverbial corridors of power in Washington.[46] The general results of this type of psychological offensive are strong indications that many "North

American" decision-makers are beginning to believe that the cost in lives and money of supporting the war in El Salvador has reached unacceptably high levels, and that the objective of a "democratic" government there is not possible or worth the price.[47]

According to Villalobos the consequent continuing demoralization of the Salvadoran society and the United States Congress, begun during the guerrilla military defensive, has and is continuing to work to the advantage of the FMLN.[48]

The forces at work within the Salvadoran government also began to shift their position during the bitter guerrilla war that took place between 1981 and 1984. As a matter of survival, they had to think and act in terms of what was absolutely necessary at any given moment. As a result, it began to be assumed more and more that the military component was the major insurgent center of gravity, and that if it were destroyed, the FMLN would lose its viability and ability to act as a meaningful force in El Salvador.[49]

Since before 1984, the government's armed efforts against the FMLN military force have been impressive. Logistically and tactically, the armed forces "have succeeded in everything (they) have set out to do".[50] They have developed the capability to move more than 50,000 troops around the country, feed them, cloth them, house them, train them, supply them with arms and ammunition, and generally sustain them better than ever. On the battlefield (since 1984) the Army has been unbeatable. In engagement after engagement, including some spectacular media events such as the November 1989 attack on the city of San Salvador itself, the guerrilla forces have been thrown back or defeated with significant losses.[51]

The Salvadoran armed forces have probably become Central America's most formidable military force. It is argued with much pride that if Nicaragua ever started a war, the Salvadorans could finish it. It is also stated—somewhat more uncomfortably—that if Honduras should again show belligerent intent, the Salvadoran military would defeat them in detail, and in short order.[52]

Those arguments may be correct, but they are also irrelevant. They point out a major reason why the Salvadoran armed forces cannot defeat the insurgent enemy it faces. The FMLN is not a conventional military force. It is not a simple collection of infantry and armor. The fact is that this or any insurgency does not have a single, military center of gravity. "It is a political organism which uses terror and other more conventional military means as only part of its arsenal."[53]

The United States has allowed and encouraged the Salvadoran security forces to grow into the image of their maker. The Salvadoran and their North American mentors have developed a conventional military force which is comfortable operating in battalion-sized formations, dependent on heavy, indirect firepower, and reliant on helicopters and trucks for mobility.[54] Indeed, they would probably be comfortable in the Fulda Gap; certainly they would be comfortable in the Chuleteca Gap.

These more conventional attributes served a useful and necessary purpose during 1981–1984 when guerrilla strategy attempted to destroy the armed forces by pitting large, more-or-less conventional FMLN units against smaller and weaker government formations. However, when that effort failed, the insurgents accepted the need for a protracted struggle. They also accepted the need to generally operate in smaller units that would emphasize hit-and-run tactics against primarily political-economic-psychological targets. Furthermore, FMLN units have avoided major confrontations with stronger government forces—except on their own terms. In short, the FMLN has adapted to the situation.

On the other hand, unwieldy conventional-type government battalions continue to expend their energy on "sweep" and "search and destroy" missions supported by fixed-wing aircraft, attack helicopters, artillery, and anti-tank weapons. This is accomplished without real purpose or results, but with great destruction and the taking of the lives of innocent bystanders. The force established between 1981 and 1986 has become largely irrelevant to the conduct of the present wars of legitimacy, subversion, and external support.[55]

This incongruous approach by the United States to organizing and equipping the Salvadoran armed forces in a generally conventional manner has complicated the task of persuading them to adapt relevant tactics and force structure to the counterinsurgency.[56] North American advisors tend to be more comfortable making recommendations on how to create better logistical or personnel management systems, or on the minor tactics of counterinsurgency. When queried as to whether these things will help win the war, they really can't answer the question.[57] The United States has not yet developed an understanding of the phenomenon and what it will take to deal with it successfully. In the meantime, without understanding or firm objectives, the hard work and operational-tactical level efforts to assist Salvadoran security forces tend to be piecemeal, misdirected, and indecisive.[58]

Finally, having shifted the strategic center of gravity away from the armed forces and back to the legitimacy of the Salvadoran government and the external support provided by the United States, the FMLN has generated a situation in which the Salvadoran armed forces "can go anywhere they want in the country". Yet, given relatively stagnant government military institutions and a less than integrated political-psychological-economic-military effort, it is obvious that the situation in El Salvador is one in which neither side has won and neither side has lost.

The result is an impasse within a protracted war. General Giap explained that in this type of war "a weak people which rises up resolutely (in the spirit of a long resistance) to fight for its freedom is sure to triumph over all enemies and to achieve victory".[59] Those who might take some satisfaction from "not having lost" to the FMLN should take little consolation.

Toward the Future: Insights, Imperatives, and Implications

There are some specific and definite things to be learned from the Salvadoran experience. One important insight at or near the top of any priority list focuses on the fundamental problem of the threat. The threat in El Salvador is multifaceted, but aimed at one objective. Speaking for the FMLN, Joaquin Villalobos explains that objective in the most lucid possible manner. He states that the guerrilla objective and thus the threat remains the same today as it was in 1981: "Our people and their vanguard are determined to win and WE WILL WIN."[60] The insurgent objective is total victory. Once internalized it provides rationale for all political, psychological, diplomatic, and military actions taken in its pursuit.

Another insight, which also ranks as one of the most important, has to do with the fact that the defeat of military forces should not be the central objective of either side in a prolonged struggle such as that in El Salvador. The primary objective of the FMLN is to destroy the legitimacy of the incumbent government and take control of the state. The primary objective of the Salvadoran government, then, must be to protect, maintain, and enhance its moral right to govern. The strategic center of gravity is the relative rectitude of the contending organizations.

The failure of the FMLN to keep this central objective in focus directly contributed to their failure to win the overall war during the 1981–1984 period. Conversely, the government during the same period recognized the importance of the legitimacy dimension. Sacrificing traditional political positions and diverting scarce resources and energies from the guerrilla war was a difficult but correct choice. Jose Napoleon Duarte understood that the people would make the final decision one way or the other.

I acknowledge that the revolutionaries may have had good reason for taking up arms when there was no hope of economic reform, social justice, or free elections. But revolution is not the act of taking power. The process of revolution may begin with a change of government, but the revolution takes place only when there has been a transformation of the economy, the social patterns, the armed forces, the education, and the culture of a country. I have had to sacrifice some values in order to provide the country a hope towards a better future. I am paying the political price today for the benefit of tomorrow. But if the Christian Democrats show that a democratic system can bring about structural changes peacefully, then the polarized choice between domination by the rightist oligarchy and violent revolution by the left will no longer be valid.[61]

The dominance of the legitimacy dimension to the general war in the case of El Salvador appears obvious. Failure on the part of the government, regardless of political orientation, to place priority on earning the moral right to govern will prolong the war, and could ultimately lead to its defeat.

Perhaps the North American corollary to the dominance of the legitimacy dimension in an insurgency is that the United States continually fails to recognize the need to organize to fight this type of conflict.[62] All the rhetoric concerning the political and psychological dimensions dominating the military dimension appears to be just that. There is no operative high-level coordinating mechanism, no "war-time" political battle staff, no special operational authority to require the State Department, the Central Intelligence Agency, the Drug Enforcement Agency, the Department of Defense, or the other "stovepipe" agencies to respond to a "low intensity conflict" problem outside of business-as-usual or crisis management channels.[63]

Instead, except for the personnel directly involved, United States' agencies continue to view the situation with complacence. Under these circumstances, it is hardly surprising that while day-to-day activities are generally handled expertly, the responses to problems tend to be reactions—short-term tactical or operational in nature, with a strong military bias. There is a virtual void in strategic perspective or vision. As General Galvin puts it:

There simply isn't enough of a unified effort of the U.S administration— the Department of State, the Department of Defense, and the other departments and agencies—somehow tied together in order to carry out a unified strategy. The organization is not there and the strategy is not there.[64]

Clearly, the final outcome of an "uncomfortable war" such as the one in El Salvador is not determined primarily by the skillful manipulation of violence in the many battles that take place once a war is recognized to have begun. Rather, the control of the situation is determined by the qualitative and quantitative levels of preparation undertaken before, during, and after the confrontation. As implications from the insights described above, several strategic requirements of this preparation could be considered as basic tenets for successful engagement in this type of conflict.

First, decision-makers and their staffs must understand the phenomenon, and therewith focus attention on solving the central strategic problem. The most refined tactical doctrine and operational art carried out by an optimum force structure in pursuit of a flawed or nonexistent strategy will be irrelevant. The realization that the nature of counterinsurgency is strategic, and that military actions within the context are politics and not simply an extension of politics by a more violent means, is a critical first step to understanding. This is a conceptual requirement demanding that planners and decision-makers begin with the formulation of strategic objectives that, if attained, will solve the root political and social causes of the conflict. Military actions can then be focused on facilitating the overall objectives, and will not become ends in themselves.[65]

As a corollary, the second requirement is to understand that legitimacy—the moral right to govern—is the central target of the insurgent. The implications should be obvious for the North American planner and decision-maker. Every action, every operation, every effort to assist a country faced with an insurgency must be taken only after it is deemed a means of assisting the incumbent regime to enhance its legitimacy.[66]

The third tenet also demands action based on an understanding of the total threat. It is primarily organizational. It is the ideal that all efforts are guided by the strategic perspective. The major implication of this tenet, borrowing from General Galvin's thoughts, is straightforward—"No organization, no strategy—no victory".[67]

Each of the above tenets focuses on strategic requirements which have long-term implications on North American ability to protect and promote its vital interests in the less developed regions of the world. To these are postulated three additional tenets which have more specific and short-term implications. They center on means by which a subversive organization might be neutralized. Moreover, these tenets require individual planners and decision-makers to take difficult but positive steps to modify force structure and provide specific skills and capabilities; to seek additional flexibility in operational authority and rules of engagement; and to reorient traditional thinking and training.

The first of this set of tenets is that intelligence is key. No situation can present a more ambiguous problem to the strategic planner or policy-maker than the indirect threats posed by an insurgency. Before, during, and after an internal crisis, there is an indispensable need to know not only the enemy, but also the "neutrals," and the strengths and weaknesses of "friends".[68]

The major implication for the multifaceted guerrilla war is that while sophisticated technical intelligence means can locate things and structured organizations, it is only through the effective use of human intelligence and psychological operations that the situations caused by people can be controlled by other people.

The second tenet in the second category is that the forces must be adaptable and actions flexible. This concept demands the realization that the type of conflict experienced in El Salvador is neither a routine, peaceful competition, nor a declared state of war. It is a different state of affairs requiring a unique set of "rules-of-engagement".[69]

The implications are significant. The national command authority and the United States Congress must begin by reconsidering the laws and procedures under which assistance is provided in this "third-state-of-affairs". At minimum, new laws, policies, and procedures must provide a capability to coordinate the commitment of resources over a long period of time and provide that assistance without forcing the assisted country to structure its armed forces and government in the likeness of the provider. In this context, the absence of "micromanagement" of specific situations, especially from afar; and the presence of a high degree of individual initiative to integrate and employ the elements that constitute power would be helpful.

The final tenet, which in many ways summarizes and sets the foundation for the others, is that there must be a proactive orientation. This is both a conceptual requirement and an all-encompassing operational requirement. To establish the ability to engage before the crisis and to efficiently assist during and after a crisis, there must be a large complement of civilian and military advisors and policy-makers who are culturally aware, politically knowledgeable, and technically prepared.[70]

This will require reallocation of priorities and funding. It will require a willingness to develop unique, coordinated planning and to develop new operational agencies. It will require the establishment of new and different sets of civilian and military career patterns. It will cost. As General Wallace H. Nutting mused in reference to all of Latin

America, "For the cost of steaming a carrier battle group up and down the coast (of Central America) for a week, we could fund most of the training programs and most of the material assistance needed for a year."[71]

The final implication is easy to state and difficult to operationalize. Ultimate success is dependent on taking those actions in a pre-crisis environment that ensure that no crisis will develop. Failing that, we need the capability to control situations such as El Salvador immediately and consistently in a planned and coordinated manner. B.H. Liddle-Hart summarizes this central concept and the others before it when he states:

> The effectiveness of armies depends on the development of methods which aim at permeating and dominating areas rather than capturing lines; at the practicable object of paralyzing the enemy's action rather than the theoretical object of crushing his forces.[72]

Conclusion

It seems to us that what we have suggested above conforms to the present realities of strategic power in the Salvadoran part of the international security arena. Thus, the operationalization of the ideas outlined above would be to produce a favorable outcome in a conflict such as that in El Salvador without a great deal of fighting. Again, writing approximately 2,500 years ago, Sun Tzu reminds us that" . . . to win one hundred victories in one hundred battles is not the acme of skill. To subdue the enemy without fighting is the acme of skill".[73]

Notes

1. Interviews with Miguel Castellanos (alias), former FMLN comandante, in San Salvador, September 1987 and February 1989 prior to his "assassination." Unless otherwise stated, interviews were conducted by Dr. Max G. Manwaring. Also see: Michael S. Radu, *Insurgent and Terrorist Groups in Latin America* (Washington, DC: Foreign Policy Research Institute for the Defense Intelligence Agency, September 20, 1984), p. 268.

2. Interviews with Dr. Alvaro Magana, former provisional president of El Salvador, in San Salvador, December 1986, June 1987, November 1987, February 1989, July 1989, and October 1989.

3. Interviews with Dr. Guillermo M. Ungo, President of the FDR, in Panama City, R.P., December 1987.

4. Interviews with Magana.

5. Interviews with Dr. Luigi R. Einaudi, Director of the Office of Policy

Planning and Coordination, Bureau of Interamerican Affairs, U.S. Department of State, in Washington, D.C., September 1987.

6. Interviews with Magana.

7. Ibid.

8. Interview with Joaquin Villalobos, Commander-in-Chief of the Revolutionary People's Army (ERP), conducted by Marta Harnecker, in Marlene Dixon and Susanne Jonas (eds.), *Revolution and Intervention in Central America*, (San Francisco, CA: Synthesis Publications, 1983), pp. 69–105; and, interview with Rafael Menjivar, spokesman for the FDR, in Ibid., pp. 63–69. Also see: Joaquin Villalobos, "El Estado Actual de la Guerra y sus Perspectivas," *ECA Estudios Centroamericanos*, No. 449, marzo 1986, pp. 169–204.

9. Interviews with General Jose Guillermo Garcia, former Salvadoran minister of defense, in San Salvador, July 1987; and, General Jaime Abdul Gutierrez, member of the civil-military junta that took control of the Salvadoran government after the 15 October 1979 coup, in San Salvador, December 1986.

10. Ibid.

11. Interviews with Magana.

12. "The Role of Unity in the Revolutionary War," an interview with Juan Chacon, former member of the Executive Committee of the FDR, in Dixon and Jonas, (eds.) Revolution and Intervention, pp. 40–46.

13. Interviews with Garcia and Gutierrez; interview with Jose Napoleon Duarte, President of El Salvador, in San Salvador, November 1987; and, Jose Napoleon Duarte, *Duarte: My Story*, (New York: G.P. Putnam's Sons, 1986), pp. 98–104.

14. Interviews with confidential C-V spokesperson. Also, according to the comments made by Castellanos and reflected in captured documentation, fully half of the young insurgent leaders' training and the major senior leadership training was aimed at preparing to fight the propaganda war. Castellanos, along with other leaders, took specific courses in Vietnam on "How to Influence the Press" and "How to Take the War to the U.S. Congress."

15. Interview with Duarte.

16. Ibid.

17. Garcia, op cit; and Gutierrez, op cit.

18. Magana, op cit.

19. Ibid.; and Einaudi, op cit.

20. Ibid.; interviews with Ambassador Deane Hinton, former U.S. Ambassador to El Salvador, in Washington, DC, September 1987; and General Wallace H. Nutting, former Commander-in-Chief, US Southern Command, in Orlando, FL, January 1987 and May 1988.

21. Interviews with Magana.

22. Harnecker interview with Villalobos in Dixon and Jonas, (eds.), *Revolution and Intervention*, and interviews with Garcia.

23. Interviews with Chacon and Menjivar in Dixon and Jonas, (eds.), *Revolution and Intervention*

24. Interviews with Colonel Joseph S. Stringham, III, former Commander, U.S. Military Group in El Salvador, conducted by Colonel Charles A. Carlton, Jr., USA, in Carlisle Barracks, PA, May 1985.

25. Interviews with Magana.

26. Harnecker interview with Villalobos in Dixon and Jonas, (eds.), *Revolution and Intervention.*

27. Guillermo M. Ungo, "The People's Struggle," *Foreign Policy*, (Fall 1983), pp. 51–63; and interviews with Ungo.

28. Ibid.

29. Duarte, *Duarte*, p. 170.

30. Interviews with Magana and Gutierrez; interviews with General Juan Bustillo, Commander of the Salvadoran Air Force, in San Salvador, January 1987; Colonel Carlos Reynaldo Lopez Nuila, former vice-minister of public security, in San Salvador, December 1986, June 1987, September 1987, February 1989, and October 1989; and, General Carlos Eugenio Vides Casanova, former Salvadoran minister of defense, in San Salvador, December 1987.

31. Interviews with Gutierrez.

32. Harneker interview with Villalobos in Dixon and Jonas, (eds.), Revolution and Intervention.

33. Interviews with Lt. General Fred F. Woerner, former Deputy Commander-in-Chief, U.S. Southern Command for Central America, in San Francisco, CA, November 1986; and, again, with General Woerner as Commander-in-Chief, U.S. Southern Command, in Panama, March 1989.

34. Interviews with Lopez Nuila.

35. Interviews with Bustillo, Garcia, and Vides Casanova.

36. Interviews with Garcia.

37. Carlton interviews with Stringham; and, interviews with Colonel John D. Waghelstein, former U.S. Military Group Commander in El Salvador, in Washington, D.C., February 1987 and January 1989.

38. Interviews with Einaudi.

39. Interviews with Magana.

40. Interviews with Ambassador Thomas Pickering, former U.S. Ambassador to El Salvador, in Tel Aviv, Israel, August 1987.

41. Interviews with Lopez Nuila.

42. Interviews with Castellanos; and, "Concerning Our Military Plans: The Military Strategy of the FMLN" (document captured and transcribed by the Atlacatl Battalion near Perquin, El Salvador, date unknown, probably late 1983, in *The Comandantes Speak: The Military Strategy of the Farabundo Marti National Liberation Front*, translated and edited by Gabriel and Judith F. Marcella, Department of National Security and Strategy, U.S. Army War College, March 1987, pp. 2–7; 19–22. Also see: "Concerning Propaganda: Our Line of Propaganda" (document presented by the Popular Revolutionary Army (ERP) at the meeting of the Command of the FMLN, July 1984), in *Ibid.*, pp. 3–8.

43. See as an example, interview with Joaquin Villalobos conducted by Ana Guadalupe Martinez, in *Semana*, 31 de octubre de 1988, pp. 6–12.

44. Interviews with Castellanos.

45. Interviews with Ungo. Also see: Joaquin Villalobos, "El Salvador Perspectiva de Victoria Revolucionaria," *Semana*, 31 de octubre 1988, pp. 18–20.

46. Interviews with Castellanos and Duarte.

47. See as an example, Charles Lane, "El Salvador: Death's Democracy," *Atlantic Monthly*, (January 1989), pp. 18–25.

48. Villalobos, "El Salvador Perspectiva."

49. Interviews with Garcia, Lopez Nuila, Magana, and Vides Casanova.

50. Interviews with General Adolfo O. Blandon, former Chief of Staff of the Salvadoran Armed Forces, in San Salvador, July 1987, September 1987, and October 1989.

51. Ibid.

52. Interviews with C-V Spokesperson.

53. Interviews with Lopez Nuila.

54. Interviews with Colonel Lyman C. Duryea, former U.S. Defense Attache in El Salvador, at Carlisle Barracks, PA, March 1986 and January 1989.

55. Ibid.

56. Interviews with Waghelstein.

57. This assertion is pieced together from U.S. military and diplomatic sources, as well as interviews with Lopez Nuila.

58. Interviews with Nutting.

59. General Vo Nguyen Giap, *People's War, People's Army*, (New York: Frederick A. Praeger, Publisher, 1962), pp. 36–37.

60. Harnecker interview with Villalobos, in Dixon and Jonas, (eds.), *Revolution and Intervention*, reaffirmed in Martinez interview, *Semana*; and, again, in "A Democratic Revolution for El Salvador," Foreign Policy, (Spring 1989), p. 122.

61. Interviews with Duarte.

62. Interviews with Pickering.

63. Interviews with Nutting.

64. Interviews with General John R. Galvin, former Commander-in-Chief, U.S. Southern Command, in Mons, Belgium, August 1987; reaffirmed in a personal letter dated 26 July 1988.

65. Interviews with Lopez Nuila drawing on Carl von Clausewitz, *On War*, translated and edited by Michael Howard and Peter Paret, (Princeton, NJ: Princeton University Press, 1976), pp. 88–89; 618–619.

66. Sun Tzu, *The Art of War*, translated by Samuel B. Griffith, (Oxford: Oxford University Press, 1971), p. 88.

67. Interviews with Galvin.

68.   Interview with Sir Robert Thompson, former commander and advisor in Malaya, in Washington, D.C., January 1986; and, interviews with Colonel John C. Ellerson, former Commander U.S. Military Group in El Salvador, in San Salvador, September 1987. Also see: Sir Robert Thompson, *Revolutionary War in World Strategy, 1945–1969*, (New York: Taplinger Publishing Company, 1970), p. 8.

69. Interviews with Lopez Nuila.

70. Interviews with Galvin; and, interviews with Major General James R. Taylor, former Commander, U.S. 193d Infantry Brigade (Panama), in Panama City, R.P., December 1986.

71. Interviews with Nutting.

72. B.H. Liddle-Hart, *Strategy*, second revised edition, (New York: Signet, 1974), p. 333.

73. Sun Tzu, *Art of War*, p. 77.

Conclusion

Ambassador Edwin G. Corr

Growing Awareness of Low Intensity Conflict as a Threat to U.S. Interests

America's principal defense priority during the last forty years has been the management of low probability, high intensity nuclear conflict with a primary focus on Europe. Yet, ironically, nearly all the armed conflicts during that time have taken place in the Third World and have been classified as low intensity. With the exception of the tragic Vietnam experience—and in large part because of it—the United States has been slow to come to grips with this problem. We have been slow to adapt our thinking, organization, and resource allocations to high probability, low intensity conflict where our military's role is usually relatively small and indirect, and where extraordinary support is required for civilian authorities in their development efforts.

Manwaring and the other contributors to *Uncomfortable Wars* demonstrate the increased attention, comprehension, and maturing of American military and civilian practitioners with respect to the type of conflicts and hostilities that have dominated our planet since the end of World War II. Earlier serious and important efforts to understand and deal with Third World conflicts are evident, for example, in Lieutenant General James M. Galvin's efforts during the middle 1950s, the Rockefeller Report of 1958, and President John F. Kennedy's subsequent creation of the "Green Berets" to respond to threats to our security in the Third World. Also, former President Richard M. Nixon warned in a book written in 1980 that World War III had already begun and was being fought on various levels— military, economic, philosophical, political, and diplomatic—in the developing world.[1]

Nevertheless, the warnings and advice of presidential commissions and important strategic thinkers over the last 40 years have not been sufficiently heeded. The American public, government, and military establishment have been slow to adapt attitudes, laws, and institutions to cope more effectively with the high incidents and prevalence of various types of low intensity conflict.

The President's statements of 1987, 1988, and 1989 on national security strategy to the congress and to the American people dedicated significant space, attention, and policy to low intensity conflict.[2] Furthermore, former Secretary of State George Shultz, speaking to the Commonwealth Club in San Francisco in October 1988, spoke of new political complexities in "the ecology of international change" and noted that, "In this decade, I believe Americans have come to recognize that we are not likely to face either an era of total war or of total peace."[3] The 1988 Report of the Commission on Integrated Long-Term Strategy also stressed American interests in Third World conflicts, and the necessity of being able to cope with them.[4] This recognition needs to be accompanied by positive action . . . changes in our thinking, laws, and organizational structure.

Reasons for American Reluctance to Grapple with Low Intensity Conflict

Part of our difficulty in dealing with low intensity conflict has been, I believe, caused by the "World War II syndrome"—not the "Vietnam syndrome", as is so often alleged. It was World War II that created for Americans an almost total unity and commitment with regard to war. During that great conflict from 1941 to 1945, the United States felt itself to be righteously, unconditionally, and totally in a crusade to liquidate evil and thereby permit the world to continue a natural evolution and progress toward peace, prosperity, and democracy. The perceptions of the simple culpability of leaders such as Hitler, Mussolini, and Tojo, and the justice of their defeat were not muddied by the stark reality of the Third World. There, the roots of hostilities are deeply embedded in historical, social economic, and political inequalities. In those circumstances, the military resolution of conflict does not—cannot—bring lasting peace, progress, and democracy. Our struggle and defeat in Vietnam, over which there was tremendous national division and ambiguity, generally reinforced our desire to return to the World War II mind-set.

While Ambassador to El Salvador from 1985 to 1988, I was impressed by the degree to which Americans remain instilled with the World War II concept of how wars should be waged and ended. Inevitably many of the visiting congressmen and citizen groups asked: "When will the war end?" Usually, those who made this inquiry were envisioning the termination of the conflict, along the lines of V-E Day in Europe, or the signing of the Japanese peace treaty on the *USS*

Missouri whereupon hostilities came clearly and finally to a halt. I tried to explain that in the prevailing form of conflict today nothing is so neat and definitive.

Sometimes guerrilla wars do in fact end by insurgent victory, but in most cases these wars smoulder for decades. With luck, they dissipate and end as the guerrilla cause and guerrillas themselves seemingly tire and finally die of old age. More realistically, however, they are reduced over time to a tolerable, manageable level in response to government legitimization and responsible counterinsurgency measures.

Professor Stephen Sloan, a colleague of mine at the University of Oklahoma who teaches a course on low intensity conflict, argues that American governments have failed to convey to the public that the type of conflict in the Third World is generally of long-term duration. To illustrate this, I often cite the experience of the British, who, with a world-class armed force and in a period when human rights were not the political concern that they are today, required fifteen years to defeat Malaysian insurgents.

Sloan suggests that quick strike and withdrawal operations, such as Grenada and the Libyan raid, have acted as a barrier to the American public's and government's understanding that most low intensity conflicts are not quickly resolvable. He further suggests that rivalry between the executive and the Congress over foreign policy prevents long-term commitments to engage in protracted conflict. In that context, the War Powers' Act demonstrates Congress's inability to recognize that in such things as "prolonged people's wars" the commitment of military advisors or forces cannot be limited to a specific period and constantly subject to negotiation.[5]

The evolution of international law on wars, the development of our national defense and foreign policy organizations, our laws, and our national psyche are built largely on a clear distinction between "war and peace".[6] Traditionally, just as Americans have defined war and peace as mutually exclusive states, civil and military roles and organizations within our government have been clearly separated. Our laws and budgeting process prohibit mixing of civil and military functions and thereby impede cooperation, coordination, and integration of U.S. military and civilian programs. This is particularly true in the implementation of foreign economic and development assistance.

Another problem with protracted conflict is that without appropriate organization, Washington (as well as the American people) soon tires, and the priority for a specific conflict drops. It comes to be an "in-box" issue dealt with in a routine and inflexible manner on personnel assignments, resource allocations, and response time to changing time to changing events and crises. In Chapter 4 of this book, Dr. William J. Olson set forth the difficulties and frustrations in bringing about radical shifts in a large and complex bureaucracy's thinking, organization, and behavior. At the same time, he suggests a strategy and the necessity for effecting such change.

Organizational Imperatives

The same Dr. Olson succinctly described in a 1988 *Military Review* article the advances within the Department of Defense to articulate a philosophy and a set of principles for low intensity conflict. He described presidential and Department of Defense directives on this subject and the structure being created within the Department of Defense to manage low intensity conflict.[7] By inference, however, the reader grasps what has been to the present a lacking concomitant commitment by a majority of the Congress and civilian foreign affairs agencies to give low intensity conflict a similar higher priority. Such commitment would be manifested by reorganizing the civilian bureaucracy to deal better with this challenge, reallocating sufficient resources, and restructuring our laws on foreign aid so that our government can better cope with the form of hostilities prevailing in the world today and likely to continue as the dominant form of armed hostilities into the twenty-first century.

Success against (or in support of) insurgencies is only partially military. As pointed out in Court Prisk's pioneering conceptual work, the key element is legitimacy. In terms of ultimate survival and success, support for civilian authorities' efforts to establish or enhance their moral right to govern is actually more important than support for host country armed forces.

The establishment or improvement of legitimacy encompasses economic, social, judicial, political, informational, and military aspects. Its very creation demands civilian political dominance by Third World governments over their own military institutions. Helping develop a country's government to attain a higher level of rectitude than its internal and external enemies makes it imperative that U.S. Government civilian agencies and officials be properly organized and prepared to help. As Max Manwaring so cogently expressed, leaving a counterinsurgency effort primarily to American military advisors and host country armed forces ignores the reality of insurgency wars. That, in turn, undermines the very essence of military submission to a civilian authority expressing the citizen's wishes, and to the essential concept of legitimacy.

Achievement of a better American effort on the civilian side of the equation could be enhanced by Department of State reorganization to ensure the necessary level of attention, guidance, coordination, and the effective implementation that is needed. This function properly resides in the Department of State, since helping governments establish legitimacy and defeat insurgencies is an operational matter. It is the effective functioning of Third World civilian officials, along with that of their military, which will establish the legitimacy necessary to bring peace and development over the long term.

The Iran-contra affair clearly shows the advisability of locating line functions in departmental agencies—not in the National Security Council—whose role is to provide policy guidance, coordination, and the resolution of agency differences. (My view on this varies significantly with those who present well argued proposals that the National Security Council assume this line function.)

A major area where executive branch and congressional action is needed to improve United States capacity to deal effectively with most low intensity conflict situations is our foreign assistance programs, both economic and security. The current structure and relatively small size of these programs critically affect our ability to support friendly governments menaced by foreign-supported insurgencies. We spend less than 2 percent of our annual federal budget on foreign assistance. During the heyday of the Marshall Plan, when we were spending in the neighborhood of 11 or 12 percent. The current level of funding is insufficient and declining, and the efficient use of these too few funds is greatly complicated by congressionally mandated earmarks and restrictions.

Essential to the success of threatened Third World governments against guerrillas and to the earning of legitimacy and popular loyalty is the extension of government presence, programs, and services into conflict areas. This function greatly transcends the valuable military concept of an organization for "civil-military operations". It demands a better U.S. government civilian effort in support of Third World governments' development programs.

The way in which the Agency for International Development (AID) is structured, operates, and is restricted by law greatly limits its ability and capacity to support host government programs. Each insurgency situation is distinct, and support must be tailored to the circumstances. It is difficult to envision that the United States would again become directly involved in a conflict where a huge program along the lines of CORDS in Vietnam would be desirable. Something similar to the AID-supported Accelerated Rural Development (ARD) program in Thailand is more conceivable. However, an AID (or other U.S. civilian entity) supported program for conflict areas patterned on the limited American military training, advisory, and support program that has existed in El Salvador might be more likely.

Our AID mission in El Salvador, while doing a superb job in supporting macro-economic policies and development projects in non-conflict areas, was limited by political and legal inhibitions from doing all that was needed to support the host government development projects in conflict areas. Political considerations based on AID's relations with congressional critics were as impeding as the legal restraints. Yet, there is a great need for American civilian support for host country civilian agencies and military in conflict areas. This might entail the creation of a small United States agency or corps of skilled civilian foreign assistance officials who can provide advice and a continuous limited presence, but who do not necessarily make operational decisions and execute programs. Through training, advice, and provision of resources they would ensure that host country development projects in contested areas are effectively and honestly implemented.

Of equal importance is the urgent need to remove restrictions on United States assistance to police. Public security forces have major roles in combating urban guerrilla terrorism and in properly controlling legal civilian demonstrations. Correct police and judicial performance is also important to ensure human rights and a more just society.

Conditions and circumstances have changed significantly since Congress chose to ban United States aid to foreign police in 1974. First, there is a growing number of civilian democratic governments in the Third World today that are greatly concerned with police comportment and human rights., This trend was not the case when the injunction was adopted. At that time the Third World was characterized by increasing military despotism and repression. Second, given the experience of the early seventies and increased sensitivity by American foreign affairs managers about human rights, any assistance program for foreign police in any given country would be closely supervised and monitored by the ambassador. Again, this was not the situation when the AID Public Safety Program was an unwanted stepchild and often remote from managerial oversight.

Finally, the caliber and education of American police advisors today are superior to those of yesteryear. The American social revolution of the late sixties and seventies that contributed to the banning of aid to foreign police also worked a transformation in our own police. In terms of education, commitment to human rights, and political sensitivities, contemporary police advisors are an improved breed. This was clearly demonstrated by the success of the police assistance program in El Salvador, when the Congress permitted a two-year exception to the ban after guerrillas killed unarmed embassy Marine security guards dressed in civilian clothes as they ate supper in a Zona Rosa cafe.

As an American ambassador who has overseen foreign assistance programs in several countries, I can assure you that the task of coordinating all the various programs and projects of the half dozen United States department and agencies involved—in order to maximize their efficiency and effectiveness—is no small challenge. A chief of mission does not manage a single foreign aid program for the country to which he is accredited. Instead, he has a number of pockets of money from which he can authorize expenditures for very specific purposes and with many, many restrictions on how that money is spent and used. There may be great gaps in the overall national aid program (lumping together here all economic, military, narcotics control, etc. projects designated for the country), but there is practically no flexibility to transfer funds among projects or to essential areas where projects have not been approved in the long and lengthy embassy—Washington process. Moreover, any change in already approved projects (often designed and approved several years earlier and no longer appropriate for the rapidly changing environment of low intensity conflict) is also bureaucratically cumbersome and time-consuming. The entire foreign assistance effort should be given greater importance, increased in size, and revamped to streamline its functioning and effectiveness.

Where to from Here?

The current period, as we move into the twentieth century, is characterized by great change in the area of national security interests. We observe at this point Japanese and Western European economic strength playing an ever-increasing influential and leadership role on the world scene. Japanese assertiveness and that country's replacement of the United States as the number one donor of foreign economic assistance is but one example. The Europeans are moving to greater unity economically and politically and are exercising greater independence from the United States in the delicate relationships and important negotiations occurring between the West and the Soviet Union and its Warsaw Pact allies. Those very allies have demonstrated surprising independence from the Soviet Union. Relations between the United States and the Soviet Union are undergoing a significant transformation, characterized by less ideological confrontation and a return more to "traditional" forms of great states rivalries. This trend will become more pronounced should progress on eliminating or reducing nuclear weapons and conventional arms continue.

Mid-level and smaller powers are in the process of acquiring advanced weaponry. They already have resorted to the illegal use of chemical warfare. Several possess medium-range missiles. A few may already have and several are capable of producing nuclear weapons. India, Brazil, South Korea, North Korea, and Egypt have important arms industries. Japan and China could become major military powers during the next twenty years should they determine to do so. We are likely to find ourselves in a world with four or five major military powers and a number of middle-range military powers. American statesmen and strategic planners will confront an increasingly more complicated security environment than they have in recent decades.[8]

As the danger of nuclear confrontation between the eastern Soviet bloc and the NATO alliance recedes, the possibilities for conventional warfare might actually grow—both among major and mid-level military powers. Low intensity conflict—embracing insurgencies, terrorism, and narcotics-related violence—is likely to persist and perhaps even expand, although proxy conflicts between the Soviet Union and the United States might diminish somewhat. A sense by the two countries that their interests usually are not seriously threatened by insurgencies and local conventional hostilities when the other super-power is not behind and/or supporting them might cause fewer proxy confrontations. On the other hand, in my opinion, low intensity conflict involving regional and subregional states will remain the prevailing form of armed hostilities over the next couple of decades, and will have implications for American national interests. The United States must at last come to understand low intensity conflict and become better prepared to cope with it.

President Reagan in his *National Security* Strategy of the United States of 1988 cautioned that while we hope current changes in the Soviet Union augur for improved and less conflictive relations, the relationship remains largely competitive and adversarial in nature. As the Soviet Union reduces its military capability and the serious threats it poses to our national security interests at all levels, we are responding accordingly. At the same time for the immediate future, the United States must continue to develop its thinking, organization, and capacity in the area where it is most vulnerable—low intensity conflict. This book is an important intellectual step forward in better preparing and organizing the United States for such problems.

I believe that reading *Uncomfortable Wars* can help to change our outdated World War II thought patterns and to set aside distortions in our thinking about low intensity conflicts caused by the tragic Vietnam experience.

It furthers an understanding that the current era is not one of clearly defined peace or war, but a third state-of-affairs. I hope the book will thereby promote changes in our attitudes, laws, and governmental organization that will enable us to cope more successfully with armed conflicts in the developing world. If we do not, it is clear to me that cumulative lack of success in high probability insurgency war will adversely affect our national interests.

In conclusion, I repeat that Dr. Manwaring and the other authors have written an important book. The context and concept of the subject are superbly treated. The principles of coping with insurgency are uniquely and soundly set forth. The organizational imperatives are succinctly described and creatively prescribed. The discussion of operational aspects of countering insurgency, especially the emphasis on intelligence and information, is basic.

Finally, the authors' comprehension of the need for host country programs to earn citizens' loyalty and to establish governmental legitimacy is fundamental. As a result, this book makes a major contribution to American efforts to provide security in the Third World as a means of ensuring democracy, development, and our own national well-being.

I have learned from reading *Uncomfortable Wars*. I hope you, the reader, have also. I hope that you will use your influence to support the creation of the attitudinal, legal, organizational, and operational changes required for our country to protect and advance its national interests in the face of the most prevalent form of armed hostilities in the current era.

Notes

1. Richard Nixon, *The Real War*. (New York: Warner Books, 1981).

2. *National Security Strategy* of the United States, report of 1987 and 1988.

3. Secretary of State George Shultz, "The Ecology of International Change," a speech before the Commonwealth Club of California, San Francisco, October 28, 1988.

4. U.S. Department of Defense, Commission on Integrated Long-Term Strategy, Discriminate Deterrence. (Washington, Government Printing Office, January 1988).

5. Stephen Sloan, "The Reagan Administration and Low Intensity Conflict: An Enduring Legacy or a Passing Fad?" *Military Review*, (January 1990), pp.42–49.

6. J. Bacevich, James D. Hallums, Richard H. White, and Thomas F. Young, *American Military Policy in Small Wars: The Case of El Salvador*,

special report of the Institute for Foreign Policy Analysis, Inc. (Washington: Pergamon Brassy's, 1988).

7. William J. Olson. "Organizational Requirements of LIC", *Military Review*, (January 1988), pp. 8–16.

8. See *Discriminate Deterrence* for an excellent discussion of the future international security environment.

About the Editor
and Contributors

AMBASSADOR EDWIN G. CORR most recently served as the United States Ambassador to El Salvador. Currently, he is the Visiting Henry Belmon Professor of Public Service at the University of Oklahoma. He received his B.A. and M.A. degrees at that same institution, and has served as an infantry officer in the U.S. Marine Corps. Mr. Corr is a career Foreign Service Officer and has been appointed as an Ambassador by both Republican and Democratic Party Presidents. Some of his most important assignments include Ambassador to El Salvador, Ambassador to Peru, Ambassador to Bolivia, and Deputy Assistant Secretary of State of International Narcotics Matters. Ambassador Corr has written various articles and books including *The Political Process in Colombia*.

LTC JOHN T. FISHEL, USA, is Chief, Policy and Strategy Division, J-5 Directorate, United States Southern Command (USSOUTHCOM) in Panama. He received his Ph.D. from Indiana University. He has served as an intelligence officer, as a psychological operations officer, in various civil-military affairs assignments, and as Chief, Research and Assessments of the USSOUTHCOM's Small Wars Operations Research Directorate. His articles have appeared in various journals including *Military Review* and the *Journal of Interamerican Studies*. John Fishel is co-author of the two volume *Participation in Latin America*.

GENERAL JOHN R. GALVIN is the Supreme Allied Commander, Europe, and former Commander-in-Chief, United States Southern Command in Panama. He received his B.S. degree from the U.S. Military Academy, and M.A. from Columbia University in New York City, and is a graduate of the U.S. Army War College. He has served in a variety of command and staff positions, and has served as an instructor at the Colombian Military Academy and the *Escuela de Lanceros*. General Galvin has published articles and books including *The Minuteman, Three Men of Boston*, and *Air Assault*.

DR. MAX G. MANWARING is an associate with Booz-Allen & Hamilton, Inc., in Panama. He received his Ph.D. from the University of Illinois, and was a Fulbright Fellow in Brazil. He has served in various academic and military positions including the Army War College, the Defense Intelligence Agency, and the United States Southern Command's Small Wars Operations Research Directorate. Dr. Manwaring is the author of several articles dealing with Low-Intensity Conflict and Latin America, and is the senior editor of *El Salvador at War: An Oral History*.

DR. WILLIAM J. OLSON is the director of the Low-Intensity Conflict Organization of the Assistant Secretary of Defense for Special Operations and Low-Intensity Conflict. He received his Ph.D. from the University of Texas at Austin; was a Fulbright Scholar in Iran; a Leverhulme Fellow at the University of Aberdeen, Scotland; and a university fellow at the University of Sydney, Australia. He has been an research associate at the Center for Strategic and International Studies, Georgetown University, and a regional security affairs analyst at the Strategic Studies Institute, U.S. Army War College, Carlisle Barracks, Pennsylvania. Dr. Olson is the author and coauthor of several articles and books including *Guerrilla Warfare and Counterinsurgency*, and *U.S. Strategy in the Persian Gulf*.

COL COURTNEY E. PRISK, USA (Ret), is a senior associate with Booz-Allen & Hamilton, Inc., in Panama. He received his B.S. from the U.S. Military Academy, and M.A. from the University of Missouri at Kansas City, and is a graduate of the Air War College. He has served in various posts including the U.S. Army Command and Staff College, the Political-Military Affairs Division of the Office of the Joint Chiefs of Staff (JCS), and has served as the Executive Officer for the JCS Representative to the SALT II negotiations. Courtney Prisk is currently completing a new book, *The Comandante Speaks: Conversations with Miquel Castellanos*.

GENERAL FRED F. WOERNER, USA (Ret), is a former Commander-in-Chief, United States Southern Command in Panama. He received his B.S. from the U.S. Military Academy, and M.A. from the University of Arizona, and is a graduate of the U.S. Army War College. He lived in Colombia in 1965 and spent a year in study and travel throughout the northern countries of South America. He served the following three years in Guatemala as an advisor on the use of military forces in national socio-economic development. He then attended the Uruguayan Military Institute of Superior Studies in

Montevideo. He has held a variety of command and staff positions, including Deputy Commanding General, Combined Arms Training Development Activity, Fort Leavenworth, Kansas; Commanding General of the 193rd Infantry Brigade, Panama; and Commanding General of the Sixth U.S. Army at the Presideo of San Francisco, California. General Woerner is currently a professor at Boston University and a military consultant for CBS News and Booz-Allen & Hamilton, Inc.